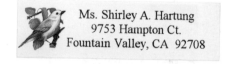

Ms. Shirley A. Hartung
9753 Hampton Ct.
Fountain Valley, CA 92708

Ms Shirley Hartung
23 Tiburon St
Napa, CA 94559

NEW YORK
FOR
NEW YORKERS

NEW YORK FOR NEW YORKERS

A HISTORICAL TREASURY AND GUIDE TO THE BUILDINGS AND MONUMENTS OF MANHATTAN

LIZA M. GREENE

W.W. NORTON & COMPANY
NEW YORK · LONDON

Library of Congress
Cataloging-in-Publication Data

Greene, Liza M.
New York for New Yorkers: a historical
treasury and guide to the buildings and
monuments of Manhattan / Liza M. Greene.
p. cm.

ISBN 0-393-03883-1

Includes bibliographical references and
index.
1. Architecture — New York (NY) —
Guidebooks. 2. New York (NY) — Buildings,
structures, etc. — Guidebooks. 3. New York
(NY) — Guidebooks. I. Title.
NA735.N5G75   1995
720'.9747'1 — dc20   95-16805

The text of this book is composed in Helvetica
Light and Helvetica Black with the display
type in Futura Extra Bold. Composition and
book design by Liza M. Greene.

Printing is by South China Printing Company,
Ltd., Hong Kong

W. W. Norton & Company, Inc.,
500 Fifth Avenue, New York, NY 10110

W. W. Norton & Company Ltd.,
10 Coptic Street, London WC1A 1PU

1 2 3 4 5 6 7 8 9 0

In Memory of Christopher Lovejoy

CONTENTS

Trinity Graveyard, *see page 2*

Castle Clinton, *see page 9*

Dakota, *see page 32*

Fiorello La Guardia,
see page 81

Chrysler Building, *see page 79*

Great Manhattan views, *see page 101*

ACKNOWLEDGMENTS

This book would not exist without the expertise offered by many individuals and publications. There is a bibliography at the back of the book and below are some of the people who provided more than generous assistance: John Baker, Ken Bergen, Debra Bershad, Louise Brockett, Jenny Brodlieb, Dan Bussolini, Sarah Carol, Rebecca Churchill, Alison Collins, Andrew Dolkart, Sarah Fleming, Gregory Gallagher, Susan Gallotzi, Tabitha Griffin, Billie Heller, Julie Hoover, Barbara Jepson, Betsy Kasha, John Kuhn, John Kriskiewicz, Barry Lewis, Chris Little, Jim Mairs, Mary McCaffrey, Jon McMillan, Meg McSweeney, Nancy Neilsen, Lauren Pack, Deb Randorf, Beth Reifers, Betty Ann Savage, Marvin Schneider, Suzanne Shenton, Mary Anna Smith, Patrick Too, Celest Torello, Susan Tunick, Alexandra Van Horne, Roger Whitney, Fred Winters.

Scaffolding covered several structures I was eager to include and thus I would like to thank the following people for the use of their photographs: Lisa Clifford for the photo of the Harlem Courthouse; Tom Flouronoy for the photo of Salmagundi Club; Polo/Ralph Lauren for the photo of the Gertrude Rhinelander Waldo House; and Kupiec & Koutsomitis Architects P.C. for the photo of the William Cullen Bryant statue. Also the American Broadcasting Company was kind enough to lend me a photo of their building, of which I just could not get a decent shot.

This book might never have been completed without the unflagging support of Robert Pondiscio who rollerbladed all over Manhattan as I peddled my bicycle in circles taking "just one more" picture. He tactfully smoothed out some of my rough prose and has since become my husband.

INTRODUCTION

Some people find New York a bit overwhelming. Some take it for granted. And there are others who overlook it entirely. This book should serve them all. My goal is to encourage you to take a fresh look at the city. I hope you will then share my enthusiasm for this spectacular place as you walk its streets.

For the sake of historical continuity, the scope of this book is limited to the nucleus of the city, the twenty-two square miles of Manhattan Island, which was virtually the extent of New York City until 1898 when the independent cities of New York, Brooklyn, Queens, and Staten Island were merged.

New York for New Yorkers is a chronological guide showing how each era of the city's past is on view today. This visual narrative uses current buildings and monuments to illustrate the ever-changing fashions and fortunes of the past. By presenting highlights of the city's history alongside the noteworthy structures of each era, I hope to offer a clear perspective on the evolution of New York.

Indeed, for a city marked by frenetic change, it's remarkable how much of old New York still stands. Throughout its history, old buildings were replaced by new ones. Gone are such architectural treasures as the old Penn Station. But where would New York be if the houses that preceded the Woolworth Building had not been razed? New York is a commercial center and has been since Peter Minuet purchased the island for trade. Thus New Yorkers expect constant change and new development. New buildings rise on the coattails of a good economy, while reuse and adaptation are the hallmarks of economic downturns. The careful observer can see the city's rich history in many of the buildings that line the streets today.

Here then is New York for New Yorkers, a mix of buildings and monuments set in the city's rich 400-year history, the built city, like no other in the world. As we move toward the next millennium, and New York's fifth century, I hope all will take another look. It is truly stunning!

Liza M. Greene
March 1995

MAP

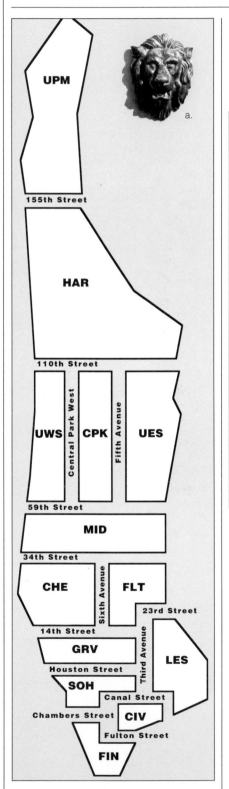

For ease in locating addresses, particularly obscure streets such as Rutherford Place or Jumel Terrace, Manhattan has been subdivided, somewhat arbitrarily, into thirteen areas, including Central Park.

KEY

●	Designated a landmark by the New York City Landmarks Commission
UPM	Upper Manhattan
HAR	Harlem/Morningside
UES	Upper East Side
UWS	Upper West Side
CPK	Central Park
MID	Midtown
FLT	Flatiron/Gramercy
CHE	Chelsea
GRV	Greenwich Village
SOH	SoHo
LES	Lower East Side
CIV	Civic Center
FIN	Financial District

EXPLANATION OF ENTRIES

Best-Known* Name of Entry
Street Address
● Each entry includes a brief description of the building or monument with a historic reference, if relevant. Often the style of the building is mentioned. If the date appears in bold in the body of the text it refers to the date that makes the structure most important. Otherwise the **bold** date at the end of the entry refers to the date the structure was completed. *Next, the architect's, builder's, or sculptor's name is in italics.* LOCation is in the bold gray type at the end.

a. Lion from Asser Levy Public Baths, *see page 59*

* Best-known name is usually the original, but in some cases a more recent name is used when the original is obscure.

1600s

Native Americans call Manhattan Manna-Hatta, Island of Hills. They are the only inhabitants until the 17th century, when Europeans begin to use it as a trading post.

1621: The West India Company, a Dutch trading group, governs New Netherland (the New York colony) until 1664.

1626: Peter Minuit, the first director general of New Netherland, trades the Reckagawawanc Indians sixty guilders ($24) worth of trinkets for the twenty-two-square-mile

Manna-Hatta and builds the first permanent settlement for 270 people.

1648: The first pier is built on the East River.

1653: The first municipal government is established with eight appointed officials. New Amsterdam is born as a mercantile proposition, not a political or religious one as were most other colonial outposts.

Giovanni da Verrazano
Battery Park
In **1524** the Florentine explorer Giovanni da Verrazano sought a new route to Asia for the king of France. The first European to enter New York Bay, he anchored and traded with the Native Americans who came alongside in their canoes. Because of inclement weather, he weighed anchor and never set foot on land. *1909, Ettore Ximenes.* FIN

The Netherland explorer Adriaen Block named a nasty stretch of the East River 'Hellegat' in 1614. The Anglicized name, **Hell Gate**, sticks. UES

Peter Stuyvesant ▲
Stuyvesant Park at East 16th Street
The one-legged Stuyvesant was considered the most able and influential of the Dutch leaders. He was the last director general of New Netherland, serving from **1647**. After nearly forty years of Dutch rule, the English took over in 1664. Instead of returning to Amsterdam, Stuyvesant chose to spend the rest of his life on his farm in NYC (see 1799). This life-size bronze statue of Stuyvesant stands on what was once part of his farm. *1936 sculpture by Gertrude Vanderbilt Whitney, founder of the Whitney Museum.* LES

In 1653, under the direction of Peter Stuyvesant, citizens built a wall across lower Manhattan to protect themselves from the English in New England. When the wall came down in 1699, the name was applied to the parallel roadway, **Wall Street**. FIN

1656: The population of the European settlement is 1,000, and there are 120 houses.

1664: The British seize New Netherland and rename it New York, after King Charles II's brother James, the duke of York.

1664: The official language is English, but residents continue to speak Dutch and eighteen other languages, including Portuguese and Hebrew.

1664: The New York colony is occupied by nearly 10,000 people, of which 1,500 inhabit NYC. New England is considerably more populated; it has 50,000 colonists.

1665: NYC's first mayor, Thomas Willett, is appointed by the British governor, Colonel Richard Nicolls.

1680s: Wealth in New York is generated from trading beaver furs until the 1680s, when greater income

is derived from the monopoly the city has on milling flour for export. The detail from an early city seal (above) reflects the importance of these trades.

1693: The first printing press in the

Trinity Graveyard
Broadway at Wall Street
● The two-and-one-half-acre cemetery includes the remains of Alexander Hamilton, Robert Fulton, and William Bradford. The oldest tombstone in the graveyard is from **1681**. Popular themes on gravestones in colonial America include the angel, the compass, the hourglass, the lamp, and the flame. A common expression on early headstones is "Remember Death," reminding visitors of their mortality. FIN

Stone Street's name came about in 1658, when it became the first paved street in the city.

The English anglicize the Dutch word for farm, *bouwerie*, to **The Bowery**. LES

First Cemetery of the Spanish and Portuguese Synagogue ▲
55 St. James Place
● This is the burial ground for the first Jewish congregation in the United States. The tombstones date from **1683** to 1825. The first Jewish settlers, fleeing purges in Brazil, arrived in 1654. LES

Broad Street, a wide, polluted canal, was filled in 1676.

Landfill has significantly broadened lower Manhattan. On the east side in the 1600s, **Pearl Street** was named for the oystershells on its water's edge. On the west side, **Hudson Street** was at the river's edge.

In the 17th century a brookside path running from Nassau Street to the East River was named **Maiden Lane** because the site was perfect for young girls to wash clothes.

Battery Place was named after a battery of artillery installed there in 1693 as protection against an attack that never came. FIN

colonies is established in New York City by William Bradford in Hanover Square.
1700: The population of NYC is 4,500.
1701: Captain William "Billy" Kidd, once a respected NYC resident and pirate hunter, is hanged in London for piracy. His wife and children remain in the city.

1702: A yellow fever epidemic strikes, taking more than 500 lives, nearly one of every nine residents.
1725: The first newspaper in New York, the *New York Gazette*, is published by William Bradford at his printshop.
1731: The population of New York City is 8,622. Ten years later the population is almost 11,000, including 2,000

slaves.
1731: A smallpox epidemic sweeps through the city, taking about 600 lives.
1731: Two hand-drawn fire trucks, NYC's first, arrive from London.
1734: John Peter Zenger, a New York publisher, is jailed for slander when he criticizes the colonial governor in his paper. The trial is popularly followed as the

right to freedom of speech is seriously tested. The not guilty verdict is celebrated in the streets of the city.

Bowling Green Park
● New York's oldest park was originally part of the Dutch cattle market, and it is popularly believed to be the place where Peter Minuit transacted his real estate deal with the Native Americans. It became a bowling green in **1733**. The fence was erected in 1771 to prevent the park from becoming a dumping ground. FIN

The Dutchman Jacob Kip built his large home in 1655 overlooking a bay in the East River at about 35th Street and Second Avenue. As the family grew, they, too, built homes in the area. By 1700 the area was commonly referred to as **Kips Bay**. The bay has long since been filled in. MID

Fraunces Tavern ▲
54 Pearl Street
● Fraunces Tavern was built in **1719** as a residence for a wealthy merchant, Étienne De Lancey. In 1762 the Georgian-style house was converted to a tavern by Samuel Fraunces, later George Washington's steward. In 1768 the New York Chamber of Commerce (see 1901) was founded here, and in 1783 Washington bade farewell to his officers here. From 1785 to 1787, it housed the departments of War, Foreign Affairs, and the Treasury. The building was reconstructed in 1907 after several fires in the 19th century. Currently a restaurant is on the ground floor, and a museum upstairs. *Original architect unknown; 1907 reconstruction, William Mersereau.* FIN

1750: Chelsea, named after the Chelsea section in London, is staked out by Captain Thomas Clarke for his estate from 14th to 24th Streets and Eighth Avenue to the Hudson River. His grandson, the author Clement Clarke Moore, subdivides the parcel into lots in 1830.

1754: Columbia University (King's College until 1784) is founded with money raised by lottery — a common fund-raising tactic.

1765: The Stamp Act is passed by Parliament to raise funds for British troops in America. After strong protests in the colonies, the Stamp Act is repealed.

1765: The Sons of Liberty, a resistance group of prominent citizens, is founded.

1766: British troops land in Kips Bay and occupy New York City until 1783. Because of the city's strategic importance, it is occupied for longer than any other city during the war.

1770: Population of New York City

Morris-Jumel Mansion
Edgecombe Avenue and West 160th Street
● This wooden house in Harlem Heights is the oldest building in Manhattan. Built in the Georgian style as a summer house for Roger Morris, a British sympathizer who fled to England when the Revolutionary War began, the house served as Washington's headquarters in 1776. It was purchased in 1810 by Stephen Jumel, a French wine merchant. When Jumel died in 1832, his widow, Eliza, remained in the house and married Aaron Burr, the eighty-year-old former vice president. Purchased by the city in 1903, it was turned into a period museum. **1765**, *John Edward Pryor.* UPM

Mulberry Street first appeared on a map in 1767. It was named after a mulberry grove on the site. GRV

St. Paul's Chapel ▲
123 Broadway
● This fine Georgian-style church is the oldest church still standing in Manhattan. Built in a wheat field, it seemed too far out of town for some parishioners, particularly since there were twenty other churches farther south. The Broadway entrance used today was originally the back door; the church was designed to overlook the Hudson. It is built of stone

and features a striking Palladian window facing Broadway. George Washington worshiped here in 1789, when New York City was the capital of the United States. **1766**, *the church is attributed to Thomas McBean; the steeple was added in 1794, James Lawrence.* FIN

TO 1783

is 20,000.
1773: The Boston Tea Party occurs. The next year a small, but similar, protest takes place in New York Harbor; eighteen cases of tea are thrown into the water.
1776: The Declaration of Independence is adopted by the Continental Congress. In a patriotic fury,

citizens pull down a statue in Bowling

Green of the English King George.
1776: A great fire destroys more than a fourth of NYC. Most of the buildings between Broadway and the Hudson, and nearly as far north as St. Paul's Chapel, burn.
1777: George Clinton, the first post-independence governor of New York,

serves for eighteen years. The state capital is in NYC until 1797.
1779: The first parade is made up of 400 "Volunteers of Ireland" who walk to a St. Patrick's Day feast in the Bowery.
1783: NYC's population declines to about 12,000 by the end of the War.

Nathan Hale ▲
City Hall Park at Park Place

In **1776**, during the Revolutionary War, the British captured Hale disguised as a schoolmaster. He confessed that he was spying and was hanged, reportedly at Third Avenue and 66th Street. Hale's final words were "I only regret that I have but one life to lose for my country." This bronze statue of a bound Hale was unveiled in 1893 on the 110th anniversary of the British evacuation of New York City. 1890, *Frederick MacMonnies.* CIV

Prison Window Memorial
Police Plaza

This window was salvaged from a warehouse where the British imprisoned American patriots until the Revolutionary War ended in **1783**. Currently it is displayed behind the Municipal Building. CIV

Harlem Monument
Broadway at 117th Street

● The plaque commemorates the Battle of Harlem Heights on this site. The battle was won in **1776** by Washington's troops. 1897, *James Edward Kelly.* HAR

The Murray House, once situated near Park Avenue and 37th Street, was the country home of Robert Murray. His wife Mary, a renowned hostess, and her daughters are remembered for stalling British officers with tea and good wines, long enough for American troops to regroup for the Battle of Harlem. The area has since been called **Murray Hill.** MID

FROM 1783

1783: Evacuation Day, November 25, is the date the British retreat from New York. It becomes a national holiday celebrated until World War I, when Americans cease to observe it in the hope of a successful British-American alliance.

1784: James Duane is appointed mayor by George Clinton, and he presides over the reconstruction of NYC.

1788: The doctors' riot is caused by mobs incensed by stories of graveyard robberies by medical students.

1789: George Washington is elected the first president of the United States.

1789: The Tammany Society is organized as a social and philanthropic group. The society evolves into a corrupt and powerful Democratic party machine.

1790: The population of

General George Washington
Union Square at 14th Street
The bronze statue marks the spot where the victorious Washington was met by the city's thankful citizens in **1783**, when the British evacuated Manhattan. The front leg of the horse is raised in the traditional symbol of victory. 1856, *Henry Kirke Brown.* FLT

Dyckman House
4881 Broadway
● This is the only 18th-century farmhouse left in Manhattan. It replaced a similar Dutch colonial house that was occupied by the British during the Revolutionary War and burned down in 1783, when they withdrew from New York. The house was rebuilt by the Dyckmans. Their farm grew to 450 acres, making it the largest farm in Manhattan. It is now a fully furnished period museum. c.**1784**, *unknown architect.* UPM

In 1731, twenty-eight-year-old James De Lancey was a New York supreme court judge. By the end of the 18th century the northern border of the De Lancey estate had become **Delancey Street**. In 1806, after James De Lancey died, **Orchard Street** was cut through his orchard. LES

MacDougal Street was named after Alexander McDougall, a founder of the Sons of Liberty, a major general in the Revolutionary War, and a state senator until he died in 1786. GRV

6

New York is 33,131, surpassing that of Boston. **1792: Bellevue Hospital is** established three miles north of Wall Street for the treatment of contagious diseases. **1792: The New York Stock Exchange** is formed by an agreement that twenty-four merchants draw up under a buttonwood tree on Wall Street. **1795: Yellow fever** strikes, killing hundreds of New Yorkers. Recurring episodes cause residents to flee north. Many settle in Greenwich Village.

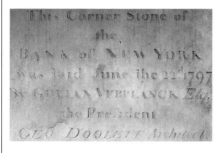

Bank of New York Cornerstone ▲
48 Wall Street
The Bank of New York was founded in 1784 by a group of men including Alexander Hamilton. The cornerstone, all that remains of the original Bank of New York, was salvaged and reset in its new building. **1789**, *unknown architect.* FIN

President George Washington
28 Wall Street
The site of this statue is one of NYC's most historic locations. It's where George Washington took the oath of office as the first president in **1789**, where the first U.S. Congress met, and where the Bill of Rights was born. The nation's capital was in New York for a year before it was moved to Philadelphia in 1790. The bronze statue was unveiled by Governor Grover Cleveland on the centennial of the evacuation of the British. *1883, John Quincy Adams Ward.* FIN

Shrine of St. Elizabeth Seton
7 State Street
● The former James Watson House (above, right) was one of a row of fashionable houses overlooking the harbor. It was begun during Washington's presidency and built in America's first architectural style—the Federal style, an interpretation of the English, more formal, Georgian style. Elizabeth Seton was born in NYC in 1774, lived here from 1801 to 1803, and was canonized as the first American saint in 1975. The columns on the addition (above, left) are said to be made from ship's masts. **1793**, *unknown architect on the original house; the wing on left added in 1806, attributed to John McComb, Jr.* FIN

In 1792 **Clinton Street** was named after Governor George Clinton. He became vice president of the United States in 1805. LES

Gracie Mansion
Carl Schurz Park at East 88th Street
● This Federal wooden house was built as a country retreat by the Scottish-born merchant Archibald Gracie. After several restorations it was acquired by the city and was home for the Museum of the City of New York from 1923 to 1932. In 1942 Fiorello La Guardia made it the first official residence of the mayor. **1799**, *unknown architect.* UES

St. Mark's Church in-the-Bowery
Second Avenue at East 10th Street
● Built on the site of Peter Stuyvesant's farm (see 1647), this simple fieldstone church contains Stuyvesant's remains. In 1828, as the Bowery became more fashionable, the church acquired the Greek revival steeple. **1799**, *unknown architect; steeple added in 1828, Ithiel Town.* LES

Abigail Adams Smith House
421 East 61st Street
● Colonel William Smith and his wife, Abigail Adams, daughter of President John Adams, built this carriage house on their large estate. By 1826 it was converted to an inn and later to a private residence. In 1924, after a period of decline, the Colonial Dames of America purchased the house, filled it with colonial furniture, and opened it as a museum. **1799**, *unknown architect.* UES

Houston Street, on the map by 1808, was a corruption of the name William Houstoun, a Georgia delegate to the Continental Congress who married a wealthy New Yorker. SOH celebrated in New York with a holiday. **1804: Alexander Hamilton** is mortally wounded in a duel with his political rival Aaron Burr.

The duel takes place in Weehawken, New Jersey. **1807: "Gotham"** is coined by the author Washington Irving as a nickname for NYC. **1807: Robert**

Fulton's 150-foot *Clermont* runs from NYC to Albany at four miles per hour, demonstrating the reliability of steam-powered boats. **1807: Importing**

slaves into the United States is outlawed by Congress. **1808: The first fire hydrant** is installed. **1808: The first public school** opens on Chatham Street.

Hamilton Grange
287 Convent Avenue
● This two-story wooden clapboard house was the country home of the statesman Alexander Hamilton. It's named after the Scottish ancestral seat of his family. **1802**, *John McComb, Jr.* HAR

Stuyvesant-Fish House
21 Stuyvesant Street
● Governor Peter Stuyvesant's great-grandson built this simple three-story Federal house as a wedding present for his daughter Elizabeth and her husband, Nicholas Fish. Their son Hamilton Fish, born here in 1808, became the governor of New York in 1849. **1804**, *unknown architect.* LES

Castle Clinton
Battery Park
● Built three hundred feet offshore for harbor defense, this circular fort was originally called the Southwest Battery and later renamed in honor of De Witt Clinton. After landfill attached it to the mainland, it acquired a roof and was used in 1823 as a concert hall (Castle Garden); in 1855, as an immigration center, preceding Ellis Island; in 1896, as an aquarium. The roof was removed,

and it currently serves as a tourist information center. **1807**, *John McComb, Jr., the first native-born architect.* FIN

The Revolutionary War general and brilliant strategist Nathanael Greene is the namesake of **Greene Street**, which was opened in the early 1800s. SOH

1810: The population of NYC is 96,373, surpassing Philadelphia's for the first time.
1811: The Commissioner's Plan (also called the Randel Plan) is a surveyor's grid, imposing today's street plan on the city from 14th to 155th Streets. The width of avenues averages a hundred feet;

the width of streets averages sixty feet. Lower Manhattan and Broadway were already established, so they are not affected by the grid.
1812: During the War of 1812 the port of New York is blockaded by the British for over a year. In 1814 the British capture Washington, D.C., and burn most of its public buildings, including the White House.
1814: Ferry service across the East River opens up Brooklyn for residential

---

Washington Irving ▲
40 Irving Place
Washington Irving (above), the first American author recognized in Europe, published the imaginative *Knickerbocker's History of New York* in **1809**. The character Knickerbocker became a symbol of the city. *1885, Friedrich Beer.* FLT

City Hall
City Hall Park
● The architect for City Hall was determined by a design competition; the prize was $350. This elegant late-Federal-style building was constructed in a cow pasture on the northernmost edge of the city. In a cost-cutting effort, the back of the building was finished in brownstone while the front and sides were finished in marble. It was thought that no one would ever go north of this point to see the back. In 1956 the deteriorating building was restored and faced in limestone on all sides. The interior features a fine central dome and stunning twin spiral staircases. This is New York's third City Hall. The mayor's office is on the ground floor. **1812**, *John McComb, Jr., and Joseph F. Mangin.* CIV

Schermerhorn Row
2-18 Fulton Street
● Schermerhorn Row consisted of warehouses and countinghouses (offices) that were built on landfill by the developer Peter Schermerhorn. After a period of decline the city purchased the property in the late 1960s as part of the redevelopment of the area that included the South Street Seaport. **1812**, *unknown architect.* FIN

Eldridge Street is named in honor of Lieutenant Joseph Eldridge, killed by Canadian Indians during the War of 1812. LES

Canal Street became a roadway in 1822, when a stagnant channel was filled in. SOH

As residents fled epidemics in lower Manhattan to rural Greenwich Village, businesses followed, including a number of banks. They opened offices on a street that became known as **Bank Street**. GRV

development by New York commuters.
1814: South Street is probably the busiest street in the city.
1820: The most populous city in the United States is NYC, with 123,706 people.
1820: Harlem, filled mostly with wealthy estates, is occupied by ninety-one families.
1821: The Fulton Fish Market is established.
1823: Clement C. Moore's "Visit from St. Nicholas" is published.
1825: The Erie Canal is finished. The 363-mile canal connects NYC to the Midwest, ensuring that New York remains the preeminent port in the New World. A great business boom ensues.
1825: Gas streetlights are introduced.
1826: Washington Square opens as a park and parade ground. The square is situated on top of a potters' field holding over 10,000 bodies. Until 1819 the city gallows were here.
1827: Slavery is abolished in New York State.

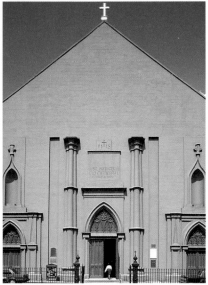

Old St. Patrick's Cathedral
260 Mulberry Street
● This was the first St. Patrick's Cathedral until the congregation began moving north (see 1879). **1815**, *Joseph Mangin; rebuilt after a fire in 1868.* GRV

Church of St. Luke in-the-Fields
485 Hudson Street
● Parishioners sailed up the Hudson to this riverside church, which was built in a rural field overlooking the river. Clement C. Moore was the first warden. **1822**, *James N. Wells.* GRV

Assay Office Facade
Metropolitan Museum of Art (see 1880)
● This classic Federal facade was from the Bank of the U.S. on Wall Street. Gold bullion was refined and formed into bars there. Dismantled in 1915, the facade was warehoused and then incorporated into the Metropolitan Museum in 1924. **1824**, *Martin E. Thompson.* UES

1830: The population of New York City is 202,589. Rural country lies north of 14th Street.
1830s: Bricks, now made by machine, look more uniform in appearance.
1830s: Shipbuilding is one of the city's major industries.
1831: Gramercy Park, modeled after a London square, is laid out on a drained marsh by the speculator Samuel Ruggles. The one-and-one-half-acre park is ringed by sixty-six lots.
1832: Asiatic cholera strikes and over 3,500 people die— 1 in 65 New Yorkers. The cholera morbus epidemic spurs growth northward as many people try to escape the disease.
1832: Horse-drawn **streetcars** replace stagecoaches and run on smooth, grade-level tracks.
1832: Seven morning newspapers and four evening papers are published in

Row Houses
127-131 MacDougal Street
These Federal-style houses were built as speculative residential properties by Aaron Burr, the former vice president. The third stories are later additions.
1829, *unknown architect.* GRV

Northern Dispensary
165 Waverly Place
Situated on a triangular base, this red-brick Federal vernacular building served as a public clinic from **1831** to 1989. In 1885, thirteen thousand people were treated here. Edgar Allan Poe was a noted patient listed in the clinic's registry. *Henry Bayard, carpenter.* GRV

NORTHERN DISPENSARY
FOUNDED 1827

In 1831 **Irving Place** was laid out and named after the New York-born author and cultural figure Washington Irving, who was at the peak of his career. FLT

In 1832 **Lexington Avenue** was named in remembrance of the the Revolutionary War's Battle of Lexington.

Washington Square North
These red-brick Greek Revival town houses were built in the **1830**s for New York's most prominent merchants and banking families, including the Delano family. Henry James (see 1881), Edith Wharton (see 1920), and John Dos Passos (see 1925) are among the better-known later residents. *Martin E. Thompson.* GRV

In 1833 a group of Greenwich Village admirers of Sir Walter Scott, who died in 1832, successfully petitioned for their street to be named **Waverly Place** after Scott's novels. GRV

NYC, each selling for six cents.
1833: The first one-penny paper, the *Sun,* is launched. It's printed with the new and efficient steampowered press.
1833: Union Square opens at the intersection, or union, of the city's two main highways: the Bowery and Broadway. The park is soon ringed by lovely residences and becomes most fashionable.
1833: Third Avenue is macadamized, from the Bowery to Harlem with a tar-based surface laid over the cobblestones.
1833: The first mayoral election takes place as a result of an amendment to the city charter. Since 1665 mayors had been appointed by the governor or a council. Cornelius Van Wyck is the first elected mayor.
1833: The Anti-Slavery Society of New York is formed in NYC.

Colonnade Row
428-434 Lafayette Street
● Behind the unifying row of columns, four of the original nine homes still exist. Initially called La Grange Terrace, after Lafayette's country estate, these were the most sought-after residences in the city. Astors and Delanos lived here until neighborhoods northward became more fashionable. The tenth president, John Tyler, married Julia Gardiner here in 1844. **1833,** *attributed to Seth Greer and Alexander Jackson Davis.* GRV

Old Merchant's House
29 East 4th Street
● Built in the most fashionable neighborhood of the day, this four-story row house was purchased in 1835 by a hardware merchant, Seabury Tredwell. His daughter Gertrude was born here in 1840 and lived here until her death in 1933. The house was built in the Greek Revival style with Federal detailing (doorway). The fully furnished interior is preserved as a museum. **1832,** *attributed alternatively to Minard Lafever and the builder Joseph Brewster.* GRV

Originally a Stable
48 Washington Mews
"Mews" is the British term for stable and service area. Here is one of a group of stables built in the **1830**s to serve the residents of Washington Square. After World War I, the stables on this charming Belgian-block street were converted to residences. GRV

Tompkins Square Park ▲
East 7th to 10th Streets and Avenues A to B
The sixteen-acre park, originally called Clinton Square, was renamed Tompkins Square Park in **1834** for Daniel D. Tompkins, a four-term New York Governor and later vice president of the United States. This statue of Tompkins is in the St. Mark's in-the-Bowery churchyard. *1939, sculptor, O. Grymes.* LES

General Theological Seminary
Ninth Avenue at 20th and 21st Streets
● The land for this seminary covers an entire city block and was donated by Clement C. Moore. The oldest of the group of Gothic Revival buildings dates from **1836**. CHE

Home of a Prosperous Man
203 Prince Street
● This Federal and Greek Revival house was built for John B. Haff, a successful leather inspector. **1834**, *unknown architect; third floor added in 1888.* SOH

New York University
70 Washington Square South
NYU, established in 1832 for the mercantile class, opened an impressive Gothic-style building in **1837**. It was demolished in 1894. This stone spire, all all that is left of the building, has been fashioned into a monument to the school's founders. It is situated next to NYU's red sandstone Bobst Library. GRV

second-largest port is New York's, second only to London's. There are sixty-three wharves on the East River and fifty on the Hudson.
1840: Brownstone becomes popular because it lends the patina of age

to the homes of the newly rich.
1840: The presidential campaign of William Harrison in NYC is run from a fake log cabin where hard cider was served.
1840: Voters no longer need to own property, but they must be white males.
1842: Water is brought forty

miles, via underground pipes and an aqueduct, to

the Croton Reservoir on 42nd Street. It greatly improves health and sanitary conditions.
1842: The City Board of Education is established to organize public schools.
1842: The Philharmonic Society is founded.

Horace Greeley ▲
City Hall Park

The outspoken reformer and renowned newspaper editor Horace Greeley launched *the New York Tribune* in **1841** and edited it for thirty years. He encouraged people to settle west of the Mississippi and is widely credited with the phrase "Go west, young man, go west." A founder of the Republican party, he was defeated by Ulysses S. Grant in the 1872 presidential election. The statue was unveiled in 1890. *Sculptor, John Quincy Adams Ward.* CIV

St. Peter's Church
22 Barclay Street

● New York's first Roman Catholic church, built in 1785, was on this site. (Catholicism was illegal under British rule.) This austere Greek Revival church features a bronze plaque honoring an early 19th-century parishioner, Pierre Toussaint, a former slave from Haiti who became a successful hairdresser and wealthy philanthropist and is now up for canonization. **1838**, *John R. Haggerty and Thomas Thomas.* FIN

In 1835 **Coenties Slip** was filled in. "Coenties" is a corruption of the name of a Dutch family that once lived nearby. FIN

In 1836 President James Madison died, and **Madison Avenue** was named for him. In the 1840s blackberry picking at the rural corner of Madison Avenue and 35th Street was popular.

CitiBank Building
55 Wall Street

● The monumental Ionic columns are a product of the new steam engine. Each was cut from a single block of stone. Occupying an entire city block, the building opened as the Merchant's Exchange; then it served as the Customs House; and later it was enlarged to house a bank. **1842**, *Isaiah Rodgers; second tier of columns added in 1907, McKim, Mead & White.* FIN

1840s: Gangs, such as the Plug Uglies, the Dead Rabbits, and the Forty Thieves, become a violent force in the slums. 1844: The Know-Nothings, formally called the True American Party, is formed. The party has a strong bias against recent immigrants and is very active in NYC. **1845: Another great fire,** covering almost the same area as in 1835, takes 30 lives and destroys 370 buildings. The combination of fires and development has eliminated much of early NYC; the street plan of lower Manhattan is virtually all that remains of the Dutch New Amsterdam. Both Philadelphia and Boston have more early

Trinity Church ▲
Broadway at Wall Street

● Built for about $90,000, this Gothic Revival structure is the third Trinity Church on this site, part of a large parcel of land granted by the queen when the church was founded in 1696. At 281 feet, the church was the tallest building in New York for nearly fifty years. The nearly black surface was cleaned in 1992 to reveal a surprisingly rosy New Jersey brownstone. **1846**, *Richard Upjohn, founder of the American Institute of Architects in 1857.* FIN

Sun Building ▲
280 Broadway

● A.T. Stewart built 280 Broadway for his dry goods store, America's first great department store. After it moved uptown, the *New York Sun* purchased the building in 1917. It has been owned by the city since 1970, but the *Sun*'s clock still graces its corner. **1846**, *Joseph Trench & John P. Snook.* CIV

Mayor James Harper Residence
4 Gramercy Park West

● Twin lanterns in front of a residence often signify that it was once a mayor's home. The lanterns made it easier at night to find the mayor's house in case of an emergency. The house on the left was once that of James Harper, mayor from 1844 to 1847. The wrought-iron work on the canopy and railing is stunning. **1846**, *attributed to Alexander Jackson Davis.* FLT

Church of the Holy Communion
47 West 20th Street

● This brownstone church was one of the first free churches in America. It was well subsidized by its wealthy congregation, until it became fashionable to live farther north. In the 1970s its congregation was merged with St. George's, and the building was sold and became a club, the Limelight. **1846**, *Richard M. Upjohn.* CHE

TO 1849

landmarks left.

1845: The Knickerbocker Club in NYC was the first formally organized baseball team in the United States.

1845: In the Five Points, a decrepit gang-invested neighborhood on the Lower East Side, the police estimate that a murder a day is committed.

1846: The Irish potato famine drives a wave of Irish immigrants to New York. NINA is a common acronym for "No Irish Need Apply" on help wanted signs through the 1860s.

1847: Madison Square park opens. It had been military drilling ground and a potters' field for yellow fever victims.

1849: The Astor Place Riot, an outgrowth of strong anti-foreigner sentiment, is ignited by the rivalry between an American and an English Shakespearean actor; 31 people die in the riot.

Grace Church
800 Broadway

● This white marble Gothic Revival church with intricate tracery was considered ostentatious when it opened. The congregation moved here from Rector Street, and it was soon the ecclesiastical center of New York society. Pews sold for as much as $1,400. As recently as 1960 some pews were still in private hands. **1846**, *James Renwick, Jr., who was only twenty-five when he received this commission in 1843.* GRV

In 1784 John Jacob Astor began as a furrier in New York. By the time he died in 1848, he was the richest man in America and was considered NYC's shrewdest real estate investor. **Astor Place**, near where he lived, was named for him. GRV

The Worth Monument ▲
25th Street and Fifth Avenue

The fifty-one-foot-high obelisk commemorates the bravery of Major General William Jenkins Worth during the Mexican War (**1846** to 1848) and marks his remains. *1857, James Goodwin Batterson.* FLT

The Arsenal
830 Fifth Avenue in Central Park

● Built by the state to store military guns and ammunition, it became city property in 1857. It served as a police station and later the first museum of natural history.

Currently it houses the Department of Park's offices. Ornament on the simple building is confined to the entry (above). **1848**, *Martin E. Thompson.* CPK

1849: An Asiatic cholera epidemic takes 5,071 lives. **1849: Mayors' terms** are extended to two years. **By 1850: Cast iron**, a new building material, becomes economically viable. It's often considered the plastic of the 19th century, and efforts are made to disguise it with faux finishes. **1850: There are 515,547 people in NYC**, more than double the population of just twenty years earlier. The city is built up solidly to 34th Street. **1850: Jenny Lind**, the "Swedish Nightingale," makes her American debut at Castle Garden (see 1807). Flattered by her warm reception, she donates the significant proceeds from the concert to NYC charities. **1850s: Places of worship**, over 250 in NYC, represent

Sniffen Court
150-158 East 36th Street
● In the **1850s** these were stables built by John Sniffen in an alley of what was once a prime residential neighborhood. After World War I the Romanesque Revival stables were converted to ten two-story town houses. **MID**

Salmagundi Club
47 Fifth Avenue
● This brownstone was built for Irad Hawley, president of the Pennsylvania Coal Company. In 1917 it became home of the Salmagundi Club, America's oldest artists' club, founded in 1871. This is one of the last unaltered brownstone facades that once lined Fifth Avenue from Washington Square to Central Park. **1853**, *architect unknown.* GRV

Marble Collegiate Church
272 Fifth Avenue
● Founded by the Dutch in 1628, this marble Gothic Revival church features a stunning spire. The world-renowned Dr. Norman Vincent Peale was the pastor for decades. **1854**, *Samuel A. Warner.* MID

nearly every denomination. **1851:** *New York Times* first appears. **1851: Herman Melville**, a native New Yorker, publishes *Moby Dick*. **1851: Burials south of 86th Street are** banned. **1852: William M. Tweed** is elected to the City Council. Over the next twenty years, with Tammany Hall (see 1789), he gains control over much of the city and state. **1853: The Crystal Palace,** America's first world's fair, opens on 42nd Street, the future site of Bryant Park. The fair runs for two seasons. **1853: The Children's Aid Society** is established in response to the estimated ten thousand children living in the streets. **1854: Over half a million Germans** come to America in two years. The 1848–1849 German Revolution precipitated the wave of immigration.

Astor Free Library
425 Lafayette Street

● With a $400,000 bequest from John Jacob Astor, New York's first free public library was built. Initially it was open only in daylight hours because it had little artificial light. Washington Irving (see 1809) was the library's first president. Now it's the home of the Public Theater. **1853**, *south wing, Alexander Saeltzer; center section, 1859, Griffith Thomas.* GRV

A Professional Man's Home
447 West 24th Street

This is one of a row of Greek Revival houses built for merchants and professional people. **1850**, *unknown architect.* CHE

McSorley's Old Ale House
15 East 7th Street

This ale house claims to be the oldest saloon in NYC. It opened in 1854 and was made famous by the painter Reginald Marsh. Until the 1970s it was a male-only bastion, in spite of its being owned by a woman. **1854**, *unknown architect.* GRV

India House
1 Hanover Square

● Built for the Hanover Bank, this commercial brownstone was later the headquarters for the New York Cotton Exchange, and for W.R. Grace and Company. For eighty years it has housed a private dining club. Harry's Restaurant is on the ground floor. **1854**, *attributed to Richard Carman.* FIN

1855: Walt Whitman's controversial collection of poems *Leaves of Grass* appears.
1857: Nathaniel Currier and James Ives form a partnership in NYC producing quality prints.
1857: Calvert Vaux and Frederick Law Olmsted, architect and gentleman farmer, collaborate on the winning entry in the Central Park design competition. A

Fire Bell Tower ▲
Marcus Garvey Park

● This is the only surviving fire tower of eleven built in the 1850 and 1860s. It became obsolete in 1879 when the telephone was introduced (see 1877). The forty-seven-foot cast-iron frame features a striking spiral staircase. c.**1856**, *attributed alternatively to Julius B. Kroehl and James Bogardus.* HAR

Haughwout Building
488 Broadway

● Commissioned by E. V. Haughwout for his fashionable store, the facade was painted in a faux marble finish to disguise the fact that it was made of cast iron. Repetition of the same cast-iron arches and columns reflects both aesthetic and economic sensibilities. This five-story Italianate-style building was considered avant-garde in its day. The first commercial safety elevator, made by Elisha Otis, was installed here. **1857**, *John P. Gaynor.* SOH

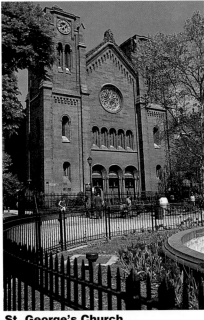

St. George's Church
Rutherford Place at 16th Street

● J. P. Morgan was so active in this church when it opened that it was often referred to as his church. The Romanesque Revival brownstone building faces Stuyvesant Square. **1856**, *Blesch & Eidlitz; Leopold Eidlitz was only twenty-three when he designed the church.* FLT

William Cullen Bryant
Bryant Park

Bryant was a cultural leader, the editor of the *New York Evening Post* for fifty years, and the primary force in **1857** behind the effort to build Central Park; as early as 1844 he had started lobbying for some pastoral relief from the city's density. This bronze sculpture was commissioned by his fellow members of the Century Association. 1911, *Herbert Adams.* MID

shantytown
and a few
thousand
squatters were
cleared from
the land on
which the park
was to be built.
1858: A

depression
spreads across
the country.
Four thousand
needy New
Yorkers are
given jobs
constructing
Central Park.

**1858: R. H.
Macy,** a retired
ship captain,
opens a dry
goods store at
Sixth Avenue
and 14th Street.
**1859: The
value of**

manufactured
items
exceeds the
value of
agricultural
products sold
for the first
time in the
United States.

Theodore Roosevelt's Birthplace
28 East 20th Street

● This is a reproduction of the 1848
brownstone where Theodore Roosevelt
was born in **1858**. He was NYC's only
native son to become a U.S. president.
The house is now a museum. *Replicated
in 1923, Theodate Pope Riddle, the first
female architect in the United States.* FLT

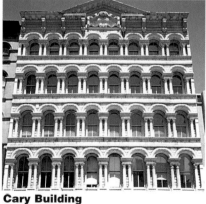

Cary Building
105 Chambers Street

● This cast-iron building served as both
a storefront and a warehouse for the dry
goods merchants Cary, Howard &
Sanger. Ornament, although liberally
used, was inexpensive because it was
made of cast iron. **1857**, *Gamaliel King
and John Kellum.* FIN

Cooper Union
East 7th Street at Astor Place

● Peter Cooper was the founder and
benefactor of the school in this Anglo-
Italianate brownstone. The school was
established for free education without
regard to race, creed, age, or sex.
Classes were offered day and night to
accommodate working people's
schedules. Mark Twain gave the
inaugural lecture in its Great Hall.
Currently it is called the Cooper Union
School for the Advancement of Science
and Art. Peter Cooper (below), the great
Victorian philanthropist and innovator,

embodies the rags-to-riches story. He
had little education, worked as an iron
maker, became partner Samuel F. B.
Morse and Cyrus Field in laying the first
cable across the Atlantic, and built the
Tom Thumb steam locomotive. **1858**,
*Frederick A. Peterson; 1897 sculptor,
Augustus Saint-Gaudens.* GRV

1860: The population of NYC is 813,669. About half of NYC's population is foreign-born; half of those are Irish. The city is densely built up from the Battery to 14th Street, but above 42nd Street there are mostly farms sprinkled with small villages, such as Yorkville, Harlem, and

Bloomingdale. 1860: Abraham Lincoln makes his famous "Right makes might" speech at Cooper Union. Nine

months later he is elected president. 1861: The Civil War causes financial speculation in all its forms. The value of goods and services nearly doubles during the war years. 1861: Mayor Ferdinand Wood proposes that New York secede from the Union to become a free city. Believing the Union would inevitably

dissolve, he doesn't want to jeopardize the city's trade relationship with either side. The idea isn't popular. 1863: The brutal Draft Riots are triggered by a new law allowing a wealthy man to pay $300 for another man to fight for him. An estimated 1,000 people are killed and

Edwin Booth ▲
Gramercy Park
Edwin Booth was America's foremost Shakespearean actor in **1864**. Facing what was once his home at Gramercy Park, he's commemorated as Hamlet. He was the older brother of John Wilkes Booth, Lincoln's assassin. The statue was commissioned by members of the Players Club (see 1888). *1918, Edmond T. Quinn.* FLT

Little Church around the Corner
1 East 29th Street
● Officially this church is called the Church of the Transfiguration. It was built in the quaint cottage Gothic style and set in a lovely garden. The grounds are entered through a lych-gate, which was common among English country churches. The purpose of a lych-gate was to offer pallbearers a place to rest with a coffin, while protecting them from the weather. **1861**, *architect unknown; 1896 lych-gate, Frederick Clarke Withers.* MID

Friends Meeting House
15 Rutherford Place
● Situated facing Stuyvesant Square, this Quaker meeting house is a spartan interpretation of the popular Greek Revival style. **1861**, *attributed to Charles Bunting.* FLT

8,000 wounded over four days of mob violence. These are the worst riots in U.S. history. **1865: Lincoln** is assassinated in Washington. He lies in state at City Hall for twenty-four hours; 120,000 people pay their respects. **1865: The Fire Department** is established. Previously the city relied on volunteer firemen from dedicated fraternal organizations. **1866: The Board of Health** is organized to combat cholera. Livestock is still herded through the streets to over two hundred slaughterhouses in NYC.

1867: The new tenement law requires that running water be available inside each house or at least in the yard.

Abraham Lincoln ▲
Union Square
Commissioned upon Lincoln's death in **1865**, this bronze statue was given to NYC by the Union League Club (see 1931), a Republican group formed in support of the Union during the Civil War. *1868, Henry Kirke Brown.* FLT

The Sherman Monument ▲
Grand Army Plaza at Fifth Avenue
The heroic gilt figure of Civil War General William Tecumseh Sherman is shown, with the allegorical figure Victory, on his historic march through the South from 1864 to **1865**. The front leg of the horse is raised in the symbolic victory stance. The statue was unveiled in 1903, *Augustus Saint-Gaudens.* MID

Admiral Farragut
Madison Square
David Glasgow Farragut, America's first admiral, fought in the Civil War. He's remembered for the exclamation "Damn the torpedoes! Full speed ahead!" during the Battle of Mobile Bay. *1881, sculptor, Augustus Saint-Gaudens, his first major commission; pedestal, Stanford White.* FLT

William Henry Seward
Madison Square
Seward, secretary of state and native New Yorker, purchased Alaska from Russia in **1867** for $7.2 million. The deal was derided as Seward's Folly. This larger than life statue portrays the first New Yorker to be honored with a public monument. *1876, Randolf Rodgers.* FLT

1869: Black Friday, September 24, is caused by Jay Gould, Jim Fisk, and others trying to manipulate the gold market on Wall Street. The market collapses. **1869: The transcontinental railway** connects NYC to the Pacific. **1869: The Suez Canal** opens in Egypt. **1870: the population** of NYC is 942,292. **1870s: Restaurants** number nearly 6,000 in the city, from the renowned Delmonico's to common oyster bars. **1870s: Elevators** forever alter the real estate market, rendering high floors more

McCreery's Dry Goods Store
67 East 11th Street
Countless columns of cast iron make up the facade of this early dry goods store. In 1971 it was converted to a residential building. **1868**, *John Kellum*. GRV

Lord & Taylor's Dry Goods Store
901 Broadway
● Lord & Taylor's, the oldest retail store in New York, was established in 1826 on Catherine Street. This five-story building was the uptown branch of Lord & Taylor's dry goods store; the older downtown store had moved to Broadway and Grand Street. Shortly after this French Second Empire style building was opened, the store introduced ready-to-wear clothes. (Previously fabric was ordered and clothes were custom-made either at the store or at home.) It consolidated its branches in the city in 1914 and moved north to Fifth Avenue and 38th Street. **1870**, *James H. Giles*. FLT

Arnold Constable's Dry Goods Store
885 Broadway
● Capped by a commanding two-story mansard roof, this was one of the first and grandest stores north of 14th Street. The original facade is of marble. The later additions are of cast iron but were painted to match the marble. The store had moved north to 34th Street by 1915. In 1961 the retailer ABC Carpet & Home moved in. **1869**, *Griffith Thomas*. FLT

valuable than low floors by offering not only ease of access, but "a view." **1870s: The typewriter** makes offices more efficient. **1870s: The**

sewing machine makes the mass production of clothes possible. **1870: The first elevated train**, the el, runs on Greenwich

Street from the Battery to 30th Street. Early els featured mahogany paneling and velvet upholstery. **1870: A pneumatic**

subway prototype is built by inventor **Alfred Beach**. Politics and Tammany Hall (see 1789) derail the project.

Residences
120 and 122 East 92nd Street
● These two charming clapboard-sided houses were built when the neighborhood was still rural. **1871** *for 122 (left); 1859 for 120 (right), unknown architect.* UES

The Tweed Courthouse
52 Chambers Street
● Formally called the Old New York City Courthouse, it's most often referred to as the Tweed Courthouse because William M. Tweed and his cronies pocketed $10 million of the $14 million construction. After dominating the city for twenty years, Tweed was brought down by the scandal in 1871. The front staircase of the Italianate-style building was gracelessly removed when Chambers Street was widened in 1942. *1878, John Kellum; after Kellum's death in* **1871** *Leopold Eidlitz completed the work according to the original drawings.* CIV

The Gilsey House
1200 Broadway
● The Gilsey Hotel was a very popular hotel frequented by the likes of Diamond Jim Brady and Lillian Russell. It was built of cast iron and stone in the French Second Empire style by the developer Peter Gilsey. From 1911 to 1977 it served as commercial loft space. In 1979 the building was converted to cooperative apartments. **1871**, *Stephen Decatur Hatch.* FLT

Belvedere Castle
Central Park
● Occupying the highest point in Central Park, this scaled-down castle is perched on a 135-foot rock ledge. It houses a portion of the National Weather Service Station. **1872**, Calvert *Vaux.* CPK

1872: Edward S. Stokes murders his business partner Colonel James Fisk over Josie Mansfield. The ensuing trials make up one of the most notable criminal cases in U.S. history. **1873: NYC expands** beyond Manhattan Island. It absorbs a small portion of the Bronx and Westchester. **1873: A depression** follows a panic on Wall Street. Many department stores are forced to consolidate and close their branches south of Houston Street. **1873: William ("Boss") Tweed** (see

Water Tower ▲
Highbridge Park at West 173rd Street
● The medieval-style octagonal water tower was the first and is the only one left in Manhattan. The tower, the Highbridge aqueduct, and the Central Park Reservoir are all that remain of the Croton water system — considered NYC's largest municipal project of the 19th century. This water system was operational until 1923. **1872**, *attributed to John B. Jervis.* UPM

Central Synagogue
652 Lexington Avenue
● A pair of onion domes top the Central Synagogue, the oldest one in continuous use in New York. In search of a building style in the 19th century, many synagogues chose this Moorish revival look. **1872**, *Henry Fernbach.* MID

In 1875 Effingham Sutton, rich from the California gold rush, organized a syndicate to promote the **Sutton Place** (formerly Avenue A) neighborhood. Regardless of his efforts, the area failed to become fashionable until the 1920s. MID

72-76 Greene Street
This building is remarkable in its detailing, especially considering it was built to serve as a lowly warehouse. Cast iron allowed the windows to be large and let in lots of sunlight at a time when most buildings had inadequate lighting at best. **1873**, *Isaac F. Duckworth.* SOH

32 Greene Street
Also built as a warehouse, this cast-iron building has a striking cornice. Most of the old cast-iron warehouses have been converted to studios and residential use. **1873**, *Isaac F. Duckworth.* SOH

TO 1876

1871), longtime Tammany Hall leader, is convicted of fraud and jailed. **1873: There are over one hundred men's clubs** with membership over fifty thousand. **1876: The** Statue of Liberty is a gift from France to the United States, on the occasion of its centennial. The United States spends nine years trying to raise money for the base.

Bethesda Fountain ▲
Central Park

● Bethesda Fountain commemorates those in the navy who died in the Civil War fighting for the Union. Located in the heart of Central Park on a formal terrace (below), it was named after a

pool in Jerusalem that was thought to have healing powers. The *Angel of the Waters* sculpture (top) is by Emma Stebbins, the first woman to receive a civic commission in NYC. She was also the sister of the parks commissioner. The walls of the steps approaching the

fountain are beautifully carved with flora and fauna (detail, above). **1873**, *Calvert Vaux and Jacob Wrey Mould.* CPK

The Old Brooks Brothers Building
670 Broadway

This is the third of five sites for the Brooks Brothers' store. Established in 1818, the store was located progressively northward, following shoppers as they moved uptown. The store's reputation was established during the Civil War when it supplied uniforms to the Union army. The Victorian building features Eastlakian decor, after Charles Eastlake, the 19th-century designer. **1874**, *George E. Harney.* GRV

Marquis de Lafayette
Union Square

During the Revolutionary War, the frenchman Lafayette served in Washington's army. The statue was built with funds raised by New Yorkers of French descent. **1876**, *Frédéric Bartholdi, who also designed the Statue of Liberty.* FLT

FROM 1876

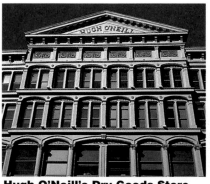

Hugh O'Neill's Dry Goods Store
655 Sixth Avenue

The cast-iron block-wide Hugh O'Neill's was a mass-market department store. Thriving for nearly forty years, the store was renowned for its aggressive sales tactics; selling sewing machines at cost, speculating that shoppers would purchase fabric and notions on the same trip. O'Neill's, one of the last great stores left in this area, went out of business in 1915. After deteriorating for a number of years, the building was refurbished and is once again the home of a large retailer. **1876**, *Mortimer C. Merritt.* CHE

B. Altman & Company
621 Sixth Avenue

Altman's was a high-quality emporium in this cast-iron building until the store moved north in 1906 to Fifth Avenue and 34th Street (see 1906). **1877**, *P. J. Jardine.* CHE

Jefferson Market
425 Sixth Avenue

In the 1830s this was the site of the Jefferson Market, one of the primary markets in NYC. This remarkable Victorian Gothic building, originally a courthouse, is now a branch of the New York Public Library. It's embellished with leaded glass, multiple roofs, and gables, plus a fanciful clock tower that once served as a fire tower. **1877**, *Calvert Vaux and Frederick Clarke Withers.* GRV

noisy and soot-spewing elevated lines. **1879: Thomas Edison** demonstrates his electric lamp in New Jersey.

1879: Gilbert and Sullivan bring their comic operas from London to New York with great success. **1879: The first telephone**

exchange in NYC becomes operative, and the first telephone directory is published; it's a card listing 252 names.

Water Tanks ▲

The pressure of the NYC water system was insufficient to deliver water above the sixth floor. Taller buildings needed water tanks and pumps. The wooden tanks have looked the same for over a hundred years, and they still present an aesthetic challenge for architects.

American Museum of Natural History
Central Park West at 77th Street
● J. P. Morgan spearheaded the building of this museum, and President Rutherford B. Hayes presided at its opening. It was considered too far north to be popular when it first opened, but

by 1898 a new wing had been added with a large central entrance for carriages. **1877**, *Calvert Vaux and Jacob Wrey Mould (only partially visible from Columbus Avenue); addition (detail, top), 1900, J. C. Cady & Co.; 1933 entrance with animal friezes (detail, above), John Russell Pope.* UWS

Stern Brothers' Dry Goods Store
32 West 23rd Street
● Here's a good example of how ornate cast-iron facades could be. The building is currently used for offices. **1878**, *Henry Fernbach.* FLT

Seventh Regiment Armory
643 Park Avenue
● This exuberant Victorian crenellated fortress is the only structure in the United States built entirely with private funds and designed to serve as an armory. The interiors were designed by Louis B. Tiffany, Stanford White, and the Herter Brothers. The armory is used for a number of exhibitions, including antiques shows. **1879**, *Charles W. Clinton.* UES

1879: The Tenant House Law of 1867 is amended to require at least 600 cubic feet of air per person and that no more than 65 percent of a lot be built on.
1879: McKim, Mead and White establish their architectural firm. They produce more great buildings than any other firm in NYC's history.
1880: The population of NYC is 1,206,299.
1880s: The most luxurious shopping area is bounded by 14th and 23rd Streets, betwe'en Broadway and Sixth Avenue. It is dubbed The Ladies Mile.
1880s: Steel skeleton

Robert Burns ▲
Central Park
Scottish residents of New York City donate this melodramatic bronze statue of the Scottish poet (1759–1796). It is located on Central Park's grand promenade, the Central Park Mall. **1880**, *Sir John Steell.* CPK

St. Patrick's Cathedral
Fifth Avenue at 50th Street
● Construction began on St. Patrick's in 1858 but ceased during the Civil War. The site was considered the outskirts of the city until the turn of the century. This French Gothic–style cathedral is the largest Roman Catholic church in the United States. More than half the stained-glass windows were made in Chartres and Nantes. The spires soar to 330 feet. The cathedral seats 2,400 people. **1879**, *James Renwick, Jr.* MID

Temperance Fountain
Tompkins Square Park
The fountain was donated by the Moderation Society to encourage the residents of the neighborhood to quench their thirst with fresh water rather than the ever-popular alcohol. The classical figure Hebe, the water bearer, rests on top. **1880**, *designed by Henry D. Cogswell.* LES

The ship *Jeannette*, outfitted by the *New York Herald* for exploration of the Arctic, was lost at sea in 1881. **Jeannette Park**, in Coenties Slip, was named in its memory. FIN

construction enables buildings to be significantly taller. This construction method does more to alter the skyline of NYC than any other technological advance.

1881: Henry James's novel *Washington Square* is published.
1881: Russian Jews are persecuted by Czar Alexander III. From 1881 to 1910 over 1.5 million Jews come to the United States;

many settle on the Lower East Side.
1881: A Harlem Yacht Club is built during a building boom in Harlem that began when the Third Avenue el reached 129th Street.

The Obelisk
Central Park, behind the Metropolitan
The 3,000-year-old pink granite obelisk from Heliopolis, erected in Central Park in **1881**, is seventy-one feet tall. It's difficult to determine the true circumstances of how the obelisk came to be in NYC. Scenario one: It was a gift from the khedive of Egypt in 1869 as thanks for America's help in building the Suez Canal. Scenario two: It was taken by William H. Vanderbilt against the wishes of the Egyptians. CPK

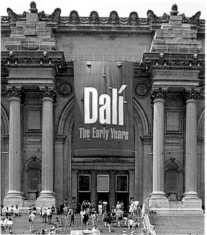

Metropolitan Museum of Art
1000 Fifth Avenue at 82nd Street
● When the museum was opened by President Rutherford Hayes, it was a red-brick Victorian Gothic building facing Central Park. Fifteen years later the entrance was reoriented to face Fifth Avenue. After six additions and many renovations, the museum contains more than thirty-two acres of floor space, making it the largest art museum in the Western Hemisphere. One barely notices that the facade is incomplete; the blocks of stones over the pairs of columns (above) were meant to be sculptures. The building and the land are owned by the city; the collections are held in trust by the trustees. The first of the museum's collections was organized in 1870 by the Union League Club (see 1931) and shown on 14th Street. In 1913 the bulk of J. P. Morgan's art collection, then valued at $60 million, made up the largest gift to the Metropolitan Museum. **1880**, *Calvert Vaux and Jacob Wrey Mould; current facade,1902, Richard Morris Hunt.* UES

W. J. Sloan's Store
888 Broadway
The terra-cotta capitals on W. J. Sloan's are delightful. The six-story brick building was where the wealthy once purchased their carpets. In 1981 the building was purchased by ABC Carpet and Home. **1881**, *W. Wheeler Smith.* FLT

FROM 1881

1880s:
Sweatshops
proliferate,
especially on
the Lower
East Side.
Immigrant
labor is willing

to work long
hours for little
pay.
**1882: An
electric
generating
plant** opens on
Pearl Street.

Electric street-
lights begin to
replace gas
lights and
lamplighters.
**1883: Mr. and
Mrs. W. K.
Vanderbilt** hold

Dakota Apartments
1 West 72nd Street
● This eight-story building was one of the first major investments on the Upper West Side. The yellow-brick and terra-cotta Dakota, one of the city's first luxury apartment houses, is an eclectic combination of gables, dormers, and arches embellished with both Gothic and Western motifs. It is surrounded by

a moat and iron rail punctuated with Zeus and sea monsters (detail above). The Dakota was home of the fictitious Si Morley from the book *Time and Again* and of many well-known personalities, including Leonard Bernstein, Roberta Flack, and John Lennon, who was shot at its entrance in 1980. **1881**, *Henry J. Hardenbergh.* UWS

President Chester A. Arthur ▲
Madison Square
In **1881**, upon the assassination of President James A. Garfield, Vice President Arthur is sworn in as president at his home, 123 Lexington Avenue. He was the second president to be sworn in in NYC; Washington was the first. *1899, sculptor, George Edwin Bissell.* FLT

Sylvan Terrace
Between West 160th and 162nd Streets
Sylvan Terrace is lined with virtually identical two-story wooden houses. The wooden canopies over the doorways are very rare in New York. **1882**, *Gilbert Robinson, Jr.* UPM

The Century Building
33 East 17th Street
● Queen Anne–style commercial buildings are rare in NYC and this deteriorating seven-story one is under renovation. It was once the home of the Century Company, publishers of the popular *Century* and *St. Nicholas* magazines and books by Edith Wharton, Mark Twain, and Rudyard Kipling. **1881**, *William Schickel.* FLT

their renowned ball for the 400 most socially prominent members of society in their new chateau on Fifth Avenue.

The number of guests is determined by the size of their ballroom. **1883: The first cooperative apartment**

building is at 34 Gramercy Park East. **1884: The Police Department** is reorganized as a civil service.

Chelsea Hotel ▲
222 West 23rd Street

● The Chelsea Hotel was one of the earliest cooperative apartment buildings. The eleven-story Victorian Gothic building became a hotel in 1905, but it still has a number of permanent tenants. The unique wrought-iron balconies (detail, top) unify the facade. The Chelsea has long been associated with people in the arts, including Dylan Thomas, Eugene O'Neill, and Thomas Wolfe. Perhaps it's most ill renowned for Sid Vicious, of the Sex Pistols, who killed his girlfriend Nancy here in 1988. **1883**, *Hubert, Pirsson & Co.* CHE

Brooklyn Bridge
City Hall Park

● The plans for this bridge were considered a folly in 1855, but residents of Brooklyn championed the cause after the Civil War. Under construction for sixteen years, it formally opened in **1883** with President Chester Arthur's walk across it. This was the first bridge over the East River and the world's longest suspension bridge, spanning nearly sixteen hundred feet. *Designed by John A. Roebling and built by his son, Washington.* CIV

Potter Building
38 Park Row

● This was the first office building with an elevator. The eleven-story, exuberant facade is decorated with cast and pressed terra cotta. It's now a residential co-op. **1883**, *Nathan G. Starkweather.* CIV

Villard House
457 Madison Avenue

● Henry Villard, the journalist and financier who became the publisher of the New York *Evening Post*, modeled these brownstone houses on a 15th-century Italian palazzo. The north and south wings were added later. In the 1980s the air rights were sold, and Villard House was incorporated into Helmsley's Palace Hotel. **1884**, *McKim, Mead & White.* MID

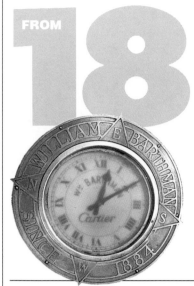

1884: Bryant Park on 42nd Street, once a Civil War drilling ground and site of the Crystal Palace, is named in honor of the cultural leader William Cullen Bryant. **1885: Ulysses S. Grant's** funeral (see 1897), one of

Barthman Sidewalk Clock ▲
174 Broadway
Set in the pavement in front of William Barthman Jewelers, the glass on the face of the clock wears quickly and is replaced every six months. **1884**, *mechanism by Cartier.* FIN

National Arts Club
15 Gramercy Park South
● In 1863 Samuel J. Tilden bought a brownstone, and in 1874, when he became governor, he bought its neighbor. Tilden was a candidate for the presidency in 1876; although he won the popular vote, Rutherford B. Hayes won the electoral vote. In 1881 Tilden commissioned Calvert Vaux to unify the two houses into one residence. By **1884** the sweeping renovation, complete with a Victorian Gothic facade, was finished. In 1906 the National Arts Club, established for artists and those supporting the arts, bought the building for its clubhouse. *Original architect, unknown; 1884 renovation, Calvert Vaux.* FLT

Western Union Building
186 Fifth Avenue
● Facing Union Square this is one of Fifth Avenue's earliest commercial buildings. **1884**, *Henry J. Hardenbergh.* FLT

Stuyvesant Polyclinic
137 Second Avenue
● The Stuyvesant Polyclinic was a health clinic commissioned by Anna and Oswald Ottendorfer, philanthropists concerned with the welfare of German immigrants. It was called the German Polyklinik, but the name was changed during World War I because of rampant anti-German sentiment. The clinic is built of brick and decorated with terra-cotta castings of famous physicians, including Hippocrates (above). **1884**, *William Schickel.* LES

the most spectacular processions in America, stretched for seven miles down Broadway.

1886: The Statue of Liberty, Frédéric Bartholdi's 151-foot copper-clad statue, is unveiled on

Bedloe's Island (renamed Liberty Island in 1956) by President Grover Cleveland.

Church of St. Paul the Apostle
Columbus Avenue and 60th Street
The stone for this church came from the Croton aqueduct (see 1842), which had been dismantled when the water pipes to the reservoir were put underground. The simple fortresslike exterior belies the elaborate interior with works by Augustus Saint-Gaudens, Frederick MacMonnies, and John La Farge. **1885**, *Jeremiah O'Rourke.* UWS

DeVinne Press Building
399 Lafayette Street
● Because the brick walls carry the load of this building without the help of a steel frame, they are over three feet thick at the ground floor. Still, the Romanesque Revival structure is elegant in its simplicity. Theodore DeVinne was a renowned printer and founder of the Grolier Club (see 1890). **1885**, *Babb, Cook & Willard.* GRV

Puck Building ▲
295 Lafayette Street
● The original entrance is marked by a gold-leafed Puck, by Casper Buberl. The Romanesque revival building was the home of the humor magazine *Puck*. By 1918 *Puck* had folded. **1886**, *Albert Wagner; addition in 1893.* SOH

Tower Nursing Home
2 West 106th Street
● This red-brick chateau-like building was originally the New York Cancer Hospital, the nation's first cancer hospital. It was funded by John Jacob Astor. In the 1950s it became a nursing home. **1886**, *Charles C. Haight.* UWS

19th Police Precinct
153 East 67th Street
When the Florentine palazzo style meets the Victorian one, the results can be delightful. **1886**, *Napoleon LeBrun & Sons.* UES

1888: The Lower East Side houses five hundred people per acre, compared to sixty per acre in the rest of the city. 1888: The Great Blizzard tears down so many overhead wires that the city is prompted to legislate that all utilities run their wires underground. 1889: The use of brownstone in buildings goes out of style as people become more interested in

Pier A
Battery Park

● The pier features a seventy-foot tower, to which a memorial clock was added in 1919 for those who died in World War I. It peals ship's bells every half hour. Currently this is the headquarters for the New York Fire Department's Marine Division. **1886**, *engineer George Sears Greene, Jr.* FIN

The Warren Building
903 Broadway

The seven-story yellow-brick bulding is trimmed with cream-colored terra cotta. It is currently office and retail space. **1887**, *McKim, Mead & White.* FLT

Eldridge Street Synagogue
12 Eldridge Street

● The lavish facade of Moorish and Gothic styles is on one of the first major synagogues established on the Lower East Side. The exterior has been handsomely restored. **1887**, *Herter Brothers.* LES

St. Cecilia's Church
120 East 106th Street

● Intricate terra-cotta details embellish this brick church. **1887**, *Napoleon LeBrun & Sons.* UWS

conspicuously displaying their wealth. **1889: The Eiffel Tower is** built in Paris. It is taller than any structure in NYC until 1930, when the Chrysler Building (see 1930) is completed.

Bailey House
10 St. Nicholas Place

● James Bailey, of Barnum & Bailey Circus fame, built his home here when the area was still rural. It's constructed with the rough-faced stone ashlar in the Romanesque Revival style. **1888**, *Samuel B. Reed.* HAR

376 Lafayette Street ▲

● Decorated with amusing terra-cotta faces (top), this six-story commercial building is of brick, sandstone, and granite. **1888**, *Henry J. Hardenbergh.* GRV

The Players
16 Gramercy Park South

● The actor Edwin Booth (see 1864) purchased this building as a home for himself and to house the club he founded for those in his profession. In **1888** Stanford White dramatically remodeled the house, adding a balcony and unique wrought-iron work. Booth died here, and his room has been preserved the way he left it. The club was exclusively male until 1989. 1845, *architect unknown.* FLT

Grolier Club
29 East 32nd Street

● This Romanesque Revival building was the home of the Grolier Club, organized in 1884 for the promotion of the arts as it pertains to books (see 1885). It was named after the 16th-century French bibliophile Jean Grolier. In 1917 the club moved uptown. The building, now called the Gilbert Kiamie House, is owned by a NYC real estate concern. **1890**, *Charles W. Romeyn.* MID

1890: The population of Manhattan is 1,441,216. **1890s: Private clubs number nearly 300** in which it is common to have multiple memberships.

1890: Jacob Riis documents the slums in his book *How the Other Half Lives.* His prose and photography heighten dramatically the public's

Park East Synagogue
163 East 67th Street
● The exuberance of this Moorish-style synagogue is accentuated by its asymmetry. **1890**, *Schneider & Herter.* UES

Fleming Smith Warehouse ▲
451 Washington Street
● At the end of the 19th century there was a renewed interest in America's colonial history, and a number of neo-Flemish style buildings, such as this warehouse, appeared. Like many warehouses downtown, this is now a residential building with a restaurant downstairs. **1891**, *Stephen Decatur Hatch.* SOH

Century Association
7 West 43rd Street
● The Century, originally a men's cultural club, moved to this Italian Renaissance, palazzo-style building in 1891. It was the first of a number of Renaissance-style clubs built by McKim, Mead, and White, who were also club members. The club was founded for writers and artists in 1847 by William Cullen Bryant (see 1857), Asher B. Durand, and others. **1891**, *McKim, Mead & White.* MID

Carnegie Hall
57th Street and Seventh Avenue
● Andrew Carnegie, the Scottish immigrant who became an industrial magnate and philanthropist, founded Carnegie Hall. Peter Ilyich Tchaikovsky conducted the opening concert. Renowned for its great acoustics, Carnegie Hall was the home of the Philharmonic until the 1960s, when the orchestra moved to Lincoln Center. **1891**, *William B. Tuthill; restored in 1986, William Morris Hunt and Dankmar Adler, consultants.* MID

In 1890, in an effort to elevate the image of their neighborhood, the residents of northern Tenth Avenue lobbied to change the avenue's name. It became **Amsterdam Avenue** in honor of New York's first settlers. UWS

awareness of the dreadful living conditions in the slums. **1892: The Cathedral of St. John the Divine**'s cornerstone is laid (see 1911). Five years earlier its eleven acres of land were purchased for $850,000. The cathedral will be unfinished into the next millennium.

Judson Memorial Church ▲
53 Washington Square South
● The ornate Romanesque Revival church and tower were commissioned by its first pastor, Edward Judson. The church's stained glass windows are by John La Farge. For decades the ten-story brick and terra-cotta tower (above) was part of the Hotel Judson, adjacent to the tower, and frequented by well-known artists and writers. In 1933 the tower was acquired by New York University. It functioned as a dormitory and most recently was turned into an international house. **1892**, *McKim, Mead & White.* GRV

Washington Memorial Arch
Washington Square Park
In celebration of the centennial of George Washington's inauguration, a temporary wooden monument was built in 1889. It was such a hit that it was reconstructed in marble as a permanent monument. The arch features two twelve-foot sculptures of Washington (below), one in military garb and the other in civilian attire. **1892**, *Stanford White; sculptor of the general, 1916, Hermon Atkins MacNeil; sculptor of the statesman, 1918, A. Stirling Calder.* GRV

American Fine Arts Society
215 West 57th Street
● Founded in 1889, the American Fine Arts Society built in the French Renaissance style this studio and exhibition space. The Art Students League, once part of the American Fine Arts Society, has been the sole occupant since 1930. **1892**, *Henry J. Hardenbergh.* MID

1893: Stephen Crane publishes *Maggie: A Girl of the Streets,* a grim look at life in New York's slums. **1893: The World's Columbian Exposition** in Chicago promotes classically inspired and highly decorative civic

---

Christopher Columbus ▲
Columbus Circle
The seventy-foot monumental column was unveiled in celebration of the four-hundredth anniversary of the discovery of America. The bronze prows extending from the granite column represent the ships *Nina, Pinta,* and *Santa Maria.* The traffic circle was given the name Columbus Circle at the same time. Funds for this monument were proudly donated by Americans of Italian descent. **1892**, *Gaetano Russo.* UWS

Harlem Courthouse
170 East 121st Street
● Romanesque Revival meets Victorian Gothic. Until 1961 this was an active courthouse. **1893**, *Thom & Wilson.* HAR

West End Collegiate Church
West 77th Street and West End Avenue
● The Dutch Reformed Church, organized in New York in 1628, is appropriately housed in this building of mixed Dutch and Flemish Renaissance styles. The adjacent school, founded in 1638, is the oldest private secondary school in the United States. **1893**, *Robert W. Gibson.* UWS

The Cable Building
621 Broadway
● The Broadway Cable Traction Company once had a power station here. Most of NYC's cable cars ran on Broadway or Third Avenue. **1894**, *McKim, Mead & White.* GRV

architecture in
New York.
**1893: Nineteen
daily,
English-
language
newspapers**
are printed in
NYC.

Fat Tuesdays ▲
190 Third Avenue
The German eclectic-style building, home of a German-American club for years, has been a jazz club and restaurant since 1970. **1894**, *Weber & Drosser.* FLT

The Metropolitan Club
1 East 60th Street
● This was built in the popular clubhouse style of the day, the Italian palazzo. It is unclear why J. Pierpont Morgan founded this club. Scenario one: He was unhappy with the accommodations at the other sixteen clubs he was a member of. Scenario two: His newly wealthy friends were not welcome at the other clubs in town. The large clubhouse became known as the millionaires club. **1894**, *McKim, Mead & White.* UES

The Harvard Club
27 West 44th Street
The restrained Georgian-style brick and limestone building reflects the architectural style of the school's campus. This is the second home of the Harvard Club of New York, organized in 1865. Forty-fourth Street was a quiet residential street when the club and several others were built on this block. **1894**, *McKim, Mead & White.* MID

In 1893 the *New York Herald* moved to 35th Street and Seventh Avenue. The triangle of land in front of the building became **Herald Square.** MID

American Surety Company
100 Broadway
Two fifteen-foot high figures face Trinity Graveyard. The Bank of Tokyo owns this building. **1894**, *Bruce Price.* FIN

1895: Theodore Roosevelt becomes president of the NYC Police Board.

1895: William Randolph Hearst, age thirty-two, comes to New York and buys

Home Life Insurance Company
256 Broadway

● Without any precedent for how a skyscraper should look, architects began to search for an appropriate style. This fifteen-story eclectic-style building with a pyramid gable top was a very early skyscraper. **1894**, *Napoleon LeBrun & Sons*. CIV

Bowery Savings Bank
130 Bowery

● This bank in the new Classic Revival style became *the* style for banks. It was inspired by the previous year's World's Columbian Exposition (see 1893). The sculpted pediment is stunning. **1894**, *McKim, Mead & White*. LES

Protestant Welfare Agencies Building
281 Park Avenue South

The style, mostly Gothic, was created by two architects best known for their many churches. There is a lovely frieze over the main entrance (below). On the left is St. Augustine preaching to the barbarians in England; on the right is Bishop Seabury preaching to the

barbarians in America. The building was formerly the Church Missions House housing a number of charities. **1894**, *Robert W. Gibson and Edward J. Neville Stent*. FLT

Engine Company No. 31
87 Lafayette Street

● The importance placed on civic buildings is clearly shown by this firehouse in the eclectic French Chateau style. The architect Napoleon LeBrun contracted with the city to design thirty firehouses. In 1986 the building was sold to two community groups. **1895**, *Napoleon LeBrun & Sons*. CIV

the *Morning Journal.*
1895: The Bronx is annexed to New York City.

1895: The Harlem Ship Canal opens, connecting the East River to the Hudson

River north of Manhattan.

Minerva and the Bell Ringers
Herald Square

Minerva, the goddess of wisdom and invention, oversees two bell strikers. Until the old New York Herald Building was razed in 1921, it featured this bronze sculpture as part of a clock. **1895**, *sculptor Jean-Antonin Carles.* MID

Squadron A Armory Facade
Madison Avenue at 95th Street

● This brick medieval castle was built for Squadron A, a National Guard unit until World War I. It was a popular spot for polo games and horse shows. In 1966 the interior was demolished, and since 1973 what is left of the facade has hidden a school playground. **1895**, *John Rochester Thomas.* UES

Siegel-Cooper Department Store
616 Sixth Avenue

● Siegel-Cooper, housed in this Beaux Arts-style building, was one of the world's largest department stores. A fountain was featured in the center of the ground floor. On opening day an estimated 150,000 people flocked to the store; 3,000 clerks were employed here. The lovliest details are above the ground floor because shoppers arrived on the el

train one story above the street. Failing to move north to the new fashionable shopping district, the store closed by 1914. (Macy's moved to 34th Street in 1902.) **1896**, *DeLemos & Cordes.* CHE

In 1896 **Sheridan Square** was named for Philip Henry Sheridan, a brilliant major general in the Civil War. GRV

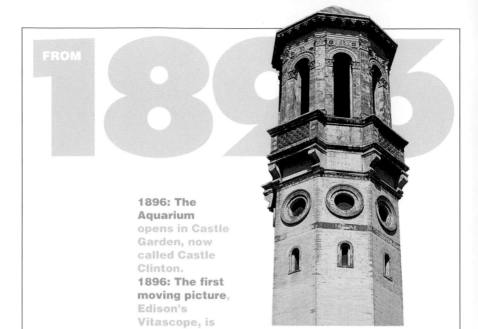

Lycée Français de New York
9 East 72nd Street
● The facade of this magnificent four-story residence is beautifully proportioned and richly ornamented. The home, commissioned in the Beaux Arts style by Henry T. Sloane, a carpet and upholstery merchant (see 1881), cost $100,000 to build. **1896**, *Carrère and Hastings.* UES

91 Fifth Avenue
● Featured on this facade are six, not particularly classical female figures (above are two). **1896**, *Louis Korn.* FLT

Church of St. Paul and St. Andrew
540 West End Avenue ▲
● An eclectic combination of German Romanesque and Italian Renaissance, this church was built of light yellow brick and features an octagonal bell tower.
1897, *Robert H. Robertson.* UWS

Shearith Israel Synagogue
99 Central Park West
● The Beaux Arts style was an unusual choice for a synagogue. **1897**, *Brunner & Tryon.* UWS

demonstrated
in NYC. It's an
instant
success.
**1896: The
gold rush**
begins in the
Klondike,
Alaska.
1896: The first

**automobile
accident**
occurs in New
York City.
**1896: The Five
Points**, the
most squalid
and notorious
housing area, is
bulldozed to

build Columbus
Park.
**1897: The first
public high
schools**—De
Witt Clinton (for
boys), Wadleigh
(for girls), and
Morris (coed)—
are opened.

General Grant's Tomb
122nd Street and Riverside Drive
● The eighteenth president of the United
States and Civil War commander
Ulysses S. Grant is entombed (not
buried; thus nobody is "buried" in
Grant's tomb) with his wife, Julia, in the
largest mausoleum in America. It's 150
feet high. Because of a lack of funds,
only one of the many proposed exterior
sculptures, *Victory and Peace* (below),

was executed. For the first decades of
the 20th century it was one of the most
frequently visited monuments in the
United States. **1897,** *John H. Duncan;
sculpture by J. Massey Rhind.* HAR

Low Memorial Library
Columbia Univesity
West 116th Street and Broadway
● The Low Library was the first building
erected on this campus. It dominates the
center of the university. Columbia, the
oldest college in New York State, was
chartered in 1754 as King's College. The
library was given by Seth Low — class of
1870, president of Columbia (1890 to
1901) and mayor of New York (1902 to
1903). **1897,** *McKim, Mead & White;
statue of Alma Mater, 1903, Daniel
Chester French.* HAR

The New Era Building
491 Broadway
● Originally built for the New Era Printing
Company, this pre-Art Nouveau, six-
story structure with a mansard roof is an
industrial loft building. **1897,** *Buchman
& Deisler.* SOH

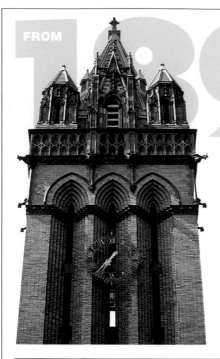

1898: Greater New York City is formed when Brooklyn, Queens, and Staten Island are politically united with New York City (Manhattan and the Bronx). This Greater New York City is 359 square miles and has a combined population of more than 3,100,000. **1898: Robert A. Van Wyck** is the first mayor of Greater New York. **1898: Fifth**

Church of the Holy Trinity ▲
312 East 88th Street

● The church, commissioned by Serena Rhinelander, was built on farmland that had been in the family since 1798. A cloister and parish house are grouped with the church amid a small garden. The lovely brick and terra-cotta bell tower, with deep Gothic arches, culminates in a cluster of turrets and pinnacles. **1897**, *Barney & Chapman*. UES

The Maine Monument
Columbus Circle

The American battleship *Maine* mysteriously exploded in Havana in **1898**. The Maine Monument honors the 260 men who died. A few months after the explosion, when Congress declared war on Spain, Cuba was a Spanish province. The allegorical figure Peace stands at the back with her arms outstretched; the youth in the prow symbolizes Cuba entering a new era. William Randolph Hearst spearheaded the fund raising for the monument. Former President William Howard Taft unveiled it. 1913, *H. Van Buren Magonigle; sculptor of figures in the boat, Attilio Piccirilli*. UWS

Gertrude Rhinelander Waldo House
867 Madison Avenue

● The leading society matron of the day, Gertrude Rhinelander Waldo, built this house in the style of a French chateau. The details and carvings (below) are

lovely. In 1986 the Polo/Ralph Lauren leased the building for one of its stores. **1898**, *Kimball & Thompson*. UES

Avenue is lined with mansions for a mile and a half above 59th Street. It is nicknamed Millionaires' Row after its wealthy residents, including the Vanderbilts, **Carnegies, Whitneys, and Fricks. The building of mansions continues until the depression in 1930. 1898: The Harlem River Speedway is opened for the running of** **horses and light carriages. It stretches for two and one-fifth miles from 155th to 198th Street along the Harlem River. This civic boondoggle costs $3 million.**

Engine Company No. 33 ▲
44 Great Jones Street
● An exuberant firehouse built in the Beaux Arts style. **1898**, *Ernest Flagg and W. B. Chambers.* GRV

Old New York Life Insurance Company
346 Broadway
Topping the twelve-story white marble skyscraper is this lovely tower with a twelve-foot-wide clock face. The stone eagles are emblematic of the New York Life Insurance Company (see 1928), which moved north to Madison Square in 1928. Since 1967 this Italian Renaissance-style building has been owned by the city. The clock has never been electrified; it's wound by hand once a week. It's one of two hand-wound clocks on the exterior of city-owned buildings— the second on the Harlem Courthouse (see 1893.) **1898**, *Stephen Decatur Hatch until his death in 1896; then McKim, Mead & White altered and completed the building.* CIV

Church of St. Ignatius Loyola
980 Park Avenue
● Built of limestone in the Roman Baroque style, the church never executed the planned two-hundred-foot bell towers, giving it a stumpy, unfinished appearance. In 1994 Jacqueline Kennedy Onassis's funeral was held here. **1899**, *Schickel & Ditmars.* UES

Augustus van Horn Stuyvesant House
2 East 79th Street
Complete with a moat, turrets, and a mansard roof, this large Gothic residence housed the last male directly descended from Peter Stuyvesant. It became the Ukrainian Institute of America. **1899**, *C. P. H. Gilbert.* UES

1899: The fashionable shopping area reaches 23rd Street and continues to expand north.

The University Club ▲
1 West 54th Street

● This is the fourth home of the University Club, founded in 1865 for "the promotion of literature and art." It was the only club of its day requiring a college degree. The exterior details on this Florentine palazzo-style building incorporate Roman motifs, including Bacchus, the god of wine (top, right), and eighteen panels corresponding to the early members' alma maters. In 1987 membership was opened to women, and by the 1990s over 230 universities were represented. **1899**, *McKim (club member), Mead & White*. MID

Appellate Division Courthouse ▲
Madison Avenue at 25th Street

● English Palladian style meets Beaux Arts decor. One-third of the building's $700,000 budget was allocated to ornamentation. The design of the courthouse was strongly influenced by the World's Columbian Exposition (see 1893). The elaborate work of sixteen sculptors was well integrated with this small-scale building. The sculptures represent real and allegorical figures in justice and law including *Wisdom* (above) by Frederick Ruckstuhl and Daniel Chester French's *Justice*. **1899**, *James Brown Lord*. FLT

The Archive
641 Washington Street

● The Archive, a massive ten-story Romanesque Revival structure, was built as a U.S. appraiser's warehouse. In 1988 it became a 480-unit residential rental. **1899**, *Willoughby J. Edbrooke*. GRV

Called the Bloomingdale Road from 59th to 155th Street until 1869, then called the Boulevard, it's finally named **Broadway** in 1899. For the first time the fifteen-and-one-half-mile road is unified with a single name. Stretching from the Battery to Spuyten Duyvil, it is the longest street in NYC.

1899: A tragic fire burns down the Windsor Hotel on Fifth Avenue and takes fifty lives.

1899: Automobiles begin to appear in NYC and are prohibited from Central Park shortly thereafter.

1899: Electric trolley cars make their appearance on the Third Avenue surface line.

1899: The Croton Reservoir at 42nd Street is dismantled.

The Park Row Building
15 Park Row

● At 386 feet this was the world's tallest building until 1908, when the Singer Building (see 1967) was completed. **1899**, *Robert H. Robertson*. CIV

Bayard-Condict Building
65 Bleecker Street

● Twelve-stories tall, this commercial loftbuilding is covered with ornate white terra cotta. The wingspan of the angels under the eaves (below) is nearly fifteen

feet. This is the Chicago architect's only New York City building. **1899**, *Louis H. Sullivan.* GRV

Lycée Français de New York
7 East 72nd Street

● The classic four-story Beaux Arts town house was designed for Oliver Gould Jennings, the industrialist and a director of Bethlehem Steel. The ornate mansard roof, copper cresting, and iron railing are stunning. **1899**, *Flagg & Chambers.* UES

New York Yacht Club
37 West 44th Street

● The sterns of sailing ships in bay windows are featured on this unique and flamboyant facade. The seven-story Beaux Arts building is on property donated by J. P. Morgan, an early commodore of the yacht club. The prestigious yachting institution was home of the America's Cup until 1983. **1900**, *Warren & Wetmore.* MID

1900: The population of Manhattan is 1,850,093; Greater New York's is 3,437,202. About 37 percent of those residents are foreign-born.
1900: Corporate headquarters of sixty-nine out of one hundred largest companies in the United States are in NYC.
1900: Nearly forty thousand manufacturing firms are in NYC. The top

Whitehall Building ▲
17 Battery Place
● With its singular top, this building was visible from the dozens of piers that once lined the Hudson River. It functioned as a control tower; tugboats received their instructions from offices in this building. The sculptural work on the facade includes devil-like characters (top). **1900**, *Henry J. Hardenbergh; addition (above) 1901, Clinton & Russell.* FIN

Theodore Roosevelt
American Museum of Natural History
Theodore Roosevelt, a native-born New Yorker, was governor of New York in **1900**, when he was elected vice president of the United States. When President McKinley was shot in 1901, Roosevelt became president. He served until 1909 and was the first, and only, NYC-born president. This bronze sculpture and the surrounding plaza were built with a $3.5 million allocation by the state legislature. 1939, *James Earle Fraser.* UWS

Adam's Dry Goods Store
675 Sixth Avenue
● Built in the turn of the century's fashionable Beaux Arts style, this building still has its large central atrium with skylights. It was one of the last large department stores to open in the Ladies Mile district. It closed in 1915. A Barnes & Nobles superstore opened on the ground floor in 1994. **1900**, *DeLemos & Cordes.* CHE

Broadway Chambers Building
273 Broadway
● This eighteen-story building is detailed with beige terracotta and brilliant spots of color on the top four floors. This pale pink-granite Beaux Arts office building was Gilbert's first major commission in NYC. **1900**, *Cass Gilbert.* CIV

five industries
are clothing,
printing and
publishing,
machine and
foundry, food,
and
chemicals.
1900: Subway

construction
begins. Workers
average twenty
cents per hour.
**1900: Block
Beautiful**, New
York's first
major tree-
planting

campaign,
begins as a
private
initiative.
Decades later
the city takes
responsibility
for the trees
along its

streets.
**1900: Working
conditions** at
the start of
this century
include a ten-
hour workday
and a six-day
workweek.

The Lotos Club
5 East 66th Street
Built for William H. Vanderbilt's
daughter, who then passed the house to
her daughter. In 1947 it became the
home of the Lotos Club, founded in 1870
by young journalists to support literature.
Samuel Clemens was an early member.
1900, *Richard Howland Hunt.* UES

Second Church of Christ, Scientist
Central Park West at 68th Street
The squat Beaux Arts church was an
early large structure on Central Park West.
1900, *Frederick R. Comstock.* UWS

Cooper-Hewitt Museum
2 East 91st Street
● With forty-two servants to maintain the
sixty-four rooms, this was the home of
one of the richest man in America,
Andrew Carnegie (see 1891). Carnegie
was a pioneer in this northern
neighborhood, preferring open space

and large gardens. He chose the more
restrained Georgian style rather than the
popular Beaux Arts one. The canopy
over the entrance (above) is more
flamboyant than the rest of the house. In
1976 the house opened as the Cooper-
Hewitt Museum. Its collection of
decorative arts was assembled by the
Cooper and Hewitt families and is now
part of the Smithsonian. **1901**, *Babb,
Cook & Willard.* UES

1901: Seth Low, president of Columbia University and ex-mayor of Brooklyn, is elected mayor of NYC. **1901: The Tenement House Act** sets minimum standards for light, air, and sanitation for tenements, occupied by 1.5 million New Yorkers. (Any apartment building without an elevator was considered a tenement.) **1901: Andrew Carnegie** gives the city

New York Chamber of Commerce
65 Liberty Street
● Until 1973 the New York Chamber of Commerce was housed in this marble Beaux Arts building. The group was organized in 1768 by twenty merchants to promote "the general interest of the colony and the commerce of this city in particular." The group was important enough in 1901 for President Theodore Roosevelt to dedicate the building. The three open spaces between the columns featured statues of famous New Yorkers by Daniel Chester French. They were removed after they had deteriorated. **1901**, *James B. Baker*. FIN

Duke-Seman's House
1009 Fifth Avenue
● One of the last great residences that once lined upper Fifth Avenue, this was built by a developer on speculation. The six-story Beaux Arts house was purchased by Benjamin N. Duke, cofounder of the American Tobacco Company. **1901**, *Welch, Smith & Provot*. UES

The Penn Club
30 West 44th Street
This Beaux Arts building began life as the Yale Club until it moved to larger quarters in 1915 (see 1915). In 1989 this building was bought for the alumni of the University of Pennsylvania. **1901**, *Tracy & Swartwout*. MID

American Broadcasting Company
56 West 66th Street
This fortress-style armory was built for the New York National Guard. American Broadcasting Companies purchased the building in 1978. **1902**, *Horgan & Slattery*. UWS

sixty-five branch library buildings contingent on NYC's agreement to stock and maintain them. **1902: Noise and air pollution** have become a problem. NYC makes an effort to control it by banning steam trains. Train lines are electrified. **1902: Carnegie Hill** becomes the name of the area near Carnegie's house at 93rd Street, the highest point on Fifth Avenue.

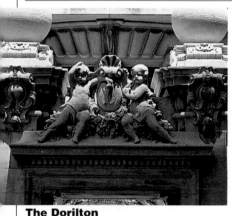

The Dorilton
171 West 71st Street

● Anticipating a housing need when the subway opened in 1904, this flamboyant French Second Empire-style building was one of the early large apartment houses to go up on the West Side. **1902**, *Janes & Leo.* UWS

St. Nicholas Russian Orthodox Cathedral
15 East 97th Street

● The Muscovite Baroque style meets the Victorian style. **1902**, *John Bergesen.* UES

Republic National Bank
452 Fifth Avenue

● This fine ten-story Beaux Arts-style building was home of the Knox Hat Company. The building was bought by the Republic National Bank in 1964 and integrated with the new skyscraper behind it in the 1980s. **1902**, *John H. Duncan.* MID

The Collectors Club Building
22 East 35th Street

● The striking bay windows were added by an early owner, an art collector desiring better light. This Georgian Revival home was purchased in 1937 by the Collectors Club, a philatelic society established in 1896. **1902**, *McKim, Mead & White.* MID

Soldiers and Sailors Monument ▲
Riverside Park and West 89th Street
● Modeled after a circular Greek temple, this marble Civil War monument is one-hundred feet tall. Above the twelve Corinthian columns runs the inscription "To the memory of the brave soldiers and sailors who saved the Union." **1902**, *Stoughton & Stoughton; sculptor, Paul E. M. DuBoy.* **UWS**

Flatiron Building
175 Fifth Avenue
● The 286-foot, twenty-one-story dramatic building fills a triangular plot where Broadway cuts across Fifth Avenue at 23rd Street. It was christened the Fuller Building, but it's dubbed the Flatiron for its wedge shape. Although a few other skyscrapers had been built by this date, the Flatiron's prominence has led it to be considered the start of the

Yorkville Branch, New York Public Library
222 East 79th Street
Andrew Carnegie's $5.2 million endowment for branch libraries included the building of this one. **1902**, *James Brown Lord.* **UES**

skyscraper era. The early steel case construction is clad in the Renaissance Revival style: in richly decorated limestone up to the fourth floor and in terra cotta (above) from the fifth floor to the top. Madison Square lost its caché after commercial buildings like the Flatiron were erected. **1902**, *Daniel H. Burnham & Co.* **FLT**

Helen Miller Gould Stables
213 West 58th Street
Built by the eldest daughter of Jay Gould, this was one of the most elegant stables to be built in New York. **1902**, *York & Sawyer.* MID

Joseph Pulitzer's Residence
11 East 73rd Street
Built for the Hungarian-born American journalist who had bought the *New York World* newspaper in 1883. In 1934 the Renaissance palazzo house was converted to apartments. **1903**, *McKim, Mead & White.* UES

New York Stock Exchange ▲
8 Broad Street
● Looking like a classic temple, with its giant colonnaded portico and mythological figures on its pediment, the building is designed to communicate confidence and security. The pediment sculpture, entitled *Integrity Protecting the Works of Man* (detail, top) is by John Quincy Adams Ward. In 1936 a lead-covered copper reproduction of the sculpture replaced the deteriorating marble original. **1903**, *George B. Post; enlarged in 1923.* FIN

Lyceum Theater
149 West 45th Street
● The Beaux Arts facade on the oldest theater in New York features prominent neo-Baroque columns above an undulating canopy. **1903**, *Herts & Tallant.* MID

1903

1903: Enrico Caruso, the opera singer, makes his New York debut.
1903: The steerage fare from Bremen to NYC is $33.50.
1904: Times Square is the new name for Longacre Square, in honor of the *New York Times* building's arrival. The first Times Square New Year's Eve

Slocum Memorial Fountain ▲
Tompkins Square

On the way to a picnic the ferry *General Slocum* caught fire and burned in the East River in **1904**. Over one thousand passengers died, mostly German women and children from the Lower East Side. 1906, *Bruno Louis Zimm*. LES

Consulate General of the Russian Federation
9 East 91st Street

This residence was purchased in 1976 by the Soviet government and used since 1992 as its first consulate in the United States since 1942. **1903**, *Carrère and Hastings*. UES

"Little" Singer Building
561 Broadway

● Built of metal, glass, and terra cotta, this twelve-story commercial building was considered very avant-garde. The delicate ironwork and the expanse of glass foretold modern skyscraper design. **1904**, *Ernest Flagg*. SOH

Our Lady of Lourdes Church
467 West 142nd Street

In Washington Heights this church recycled parts from three 19th-century buildings: The base is from the National Academy of Design (1846-1901); the apse is from St. Patrick's Cathedral when it was remodeled; and the two front pedestals are from A. T. Stewart's home (1866-1901), then the most luxurious residence in America. **1904**, *O'Reilly Brothers*. HAR

Ansonia Hotel
2109 Broadway

● The unrestrained Beaux Arts Ansonia took ten years to build. The seventeen-story block-square building was constructed with 340 suites, in the hope that this section of Broadway would become NYC's Champs Élysées. The building's eccentric developer, E. D. Stokes, raised chickens on the roof and sold their eggs to tenants until complaints mounted. **1904**, *Graves & DuBoy*. UWS

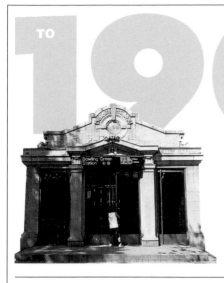

celebration takes place this year. Previously people had gathered at Trinity Church on New Year's Eve to celebrate with noisemakers after midnight. **1905: The Staten Island ferry opens.**

Battery Park Control House ▲
Battery Place

● The Dutch-style control house was one of several on the city's first subway line, the nine-and-one-half-mile IRT. The elaborate entrances were indicative of the pride the city took in its new subway system. The average worker on the construction of the subway was paid twenty cents an hour and worked ten hours a day. The cost of a ride was a nickel. The first subway system in America had opened in Boston in 1897, although a prototype had been built in NYC almost thirty years earlier (see 1870). **1904**, *Heins & La Farge.* FIN

The American Academy of Dramatic Arts
120 Madison Avenue

● The Colony Club (see 1924) was founded in 1901 by Anne Morgan, sister of J. P. Morgan. It was the first women's social group to build itself a clubhouse. It was designed in a Georgian-Federal Revival style. In 1963 it became the home of the American Academy of Dramatic Arts, which was founded in 1884 and attended by such students as Spencer Tracy, Lauren Bacall, Danny DeVito, Robert Redford, and Kate Jackson. **1905**, *McKim, Mead & White.* MID

De Lamar Mansion
233 Madison Avenue

The opulent home of the Dutch sea captain Joseph Raphael De Lamar was acquired by the Consulate of the Polish People's Republic in 1973. **1905**, *C. P. H. Gilbert.* MID

69th Regiment Armory
Lexington Avenue and 25th Street

● Built as a training center for the National Guard, this was the first NYC armory to deviate from the medieval fort model. In 1913 this was the site of the controversial "Armory Show," the international exhibition of modern art that was a turning point for American art. **1905**, *Hunt & Hunt.* MID

Diana ▲
Metropolitan Museum of Art

The sculpture *Diana* at the Metropolitan Museum is a study for the fifteen-foot sculpture Stanford White placed atop his 1881 Madison Square Garden. The public placement of the naked *Diana* was considered shocking at the time, and mothers hid the eyes of their children. In **1906** White was shot by the jealous husband of the model for the statue, Evelyn ("Peaches") Nesbit, because White had been previously involved with her and continued to flirt with her. *Sculptor, Augustus Saint-Gaudens.* UES

Cartier
651 Fifth Avenue

● In 1917 Pierre Cartier traded a rare, perfectly matched pearl necklace valued at $1 million for this house, owned by Morton Plant's widow. Upon Mrs. Plant's death in 1956, the necklace was sold for $151,000; perfect pearls were no longer as rare as they had been forty years earlier. Built in the Italian Renaissance style for the banker Plant, this is one of the last original residences left on this section of Fifth Avenue. **1906**, *Robert W. Gibson & C. P. H. Gilbert.* MID

Pierpont Morgan Library
33 East 36th Street

This simple Italian Renaissance-style building was designed for the financier J. P. Morgan to house his vast collection of early manuscripts. The library became a museum in 1924. The climactic scene of the movie *Ragtime* was filmed here. **1906**, *McKim, Mead & White.* MID

B. Altman and Company
361 Fifth Avenue

● B. Altman's was the first large retail store on Fifth Avenue (see 1877). This Renaissance Revival department store moved here from the Ladies Mile and grew to fill an entire block. In 1989 it closed. Now it houses offices and the Science, Business, and Industry Library—part of the New York Public Library. **1906**, *Trowbridge & Livingston; extended in 1913.* MID

nearly 1.3 million people arrive in the United States, the bulk of them coming through Ellis Island.

Trinity and U.S. Realty Buildings ▲
111 and 115 Broadway

● Rich in Gothic detail (top), this pair of twenty-one-story office buildings serves as a fine backdrop for Trinity Church. **1906**, *Francis H. Kimball.* FIN

Public Baths
East 23rd Street at Asser Levy Place

● Social reformers lobbied for the creation of public baths to help alleviate sanitary problems in neighborhoods where few people had bathing facilities of their own. Between 1902 and 1915, thirteen public bathhouses were built in NYC. This one featured 155 shower stalls. These baths were modeled after ancient Roman baths, and they include a prominent pair of water urns (above) framing the seal of NYC. It is now a community center. **1906**, *Brunner & Aiken.* LES

U.S. Customs House
Bowling Green

● The importance of a custom house is lost on us today; before federal income taxes were levied in 1913, customs duties were a prime source of government income. The monumental Beaux Arts building is fronted by four allegorical sculptures by Daniel Chester French representing *Asia*, *America* (shown above with an Indian, a laborer, an eagle, and the torch of progress), *Europe* and *Africa*. The statues on the sixth-story cornice portray the history of trade with cities and countries, including *Venice* (bottom left) as a doge with a gondola prow and *Spain* (bottom right), in the guise of Queen Isabella. Both are

by François Michel Tonetti. In 1973 the U.S. Customs Service moved to larger quarters in the World Trade Center. In 1994 this marble building became home to the National Museum of the American Indian. **1907**, *Cass Gilbert.* FIN

Clocks ▲
522 Fifth Avenue

● Pedestal clocks were popular when pocket watches were too expensive for most people. The clock faces often featured advertising. This nineteen-foot-tall cast-iron clock is <u>one of three</u> historic pedestal clocks left in Manhattan. **1907**, *Seth Thomas.* MID ONE IS AT THE FLATIRON BLDG, 23RD & FIFTH AVE

The Plaza Hotel
West 59th Street on the Plaza

● The Plaza Hotel opened in 1907 with eight-hundred rooms. It was remodeled in 1921, adding three-hundred rooms. It is the home of the famous fictitious six-year-old, Eloise. Both the *Great Gatsby* and *Plaza Suite* are among the numerous films that were shot here. The hotel was purchased by Donald Trump in 1988. **1907**, *Henry J. Hardenbergh.* MID

The New York Central Railroad had electrified its urban trains by 1907, enabling them to run underground. The two-and-one-half mile cut for tracks running north from Grand Central (see 1913) could now be paved over. **Park Avenue** then became a desirable residential street. Previously called Fourth Avenue, the belching smoke rendered the avenue the choice of shack dwellers. By 1924 the name Park Avenue also applied south of Grand Central to 32nd Street.

Hispanic Society of America
Audubon Terrace at 155th Street

Audubon Terrace has four small museums clustered around its bland terrace. Above is the Hispanic Society of America, as seen from the back—far more interesting than the front. The museum is filled with Hispanic paintings, sculptures, and decorative arts. **1907**, *Charles Pratt Huntington.* HAR

Regency Whist Club
15 East 67th Street

The Whist Club is a social club founded by a group of men who simply liked to play whist, a four-handed card game that preceded bridge. **1907**, *Ernest Flagg.* UES

1908

painters is derisively dubbed, opens its exhibition of realistic paintings showing NYC's gritty side. The artists include John Sloan, George Bellows, Robert Henri, and Everett Shinn.

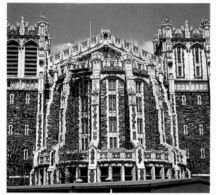

City College of New York
West 138th Street and Amsterdam Avenue
The City College of New York, founded in 1847 as a free academy, was first at 23rd Street. The complex consists of six Gothic-style buildings and is ornamented with over six hundred gargoyles. 1895-**1908**, *George B. Post.* HAR

Manhattan Bridge ▲
East River and Canal Street
This 1,470-foot bridge connects Manhattan to Brooklyn and opened the same year, equitably, as did the 1,182-foot Queensboro Bridge (top), connecting Manhattan to Queens at 59th Street. **1908**, *Manhattan Bridge, Carrère and Hastings; Queensboro Bridge, Palmer & Hornbostel; engineer for both, G. Lindenthal.* LES

The Kenilworth
151 Central Park West
This twelve-story elaborate limestone and brick apartment building overlooks Central Park. **1908**, *Townsend, Steinle & Haskell.* UWS

New-York Historical Society
170 Central Park West
● The New-York Historical Society is housed in this Classical-style building. Established in 1804, it's the oldest museum in the city. **1908**, *York & Sawyer, central portion.* UWS

1909: One of the first successful strikes is organized at the Triangle Shirtwaist Company. **1909: Wilbur Wright** makes

Felix M. Warburg House
1109 Fifth Avenue
● The French Renaissance chateau-style home was built for the banker Felix Warburg (whom the character Daddy Warbucks was modeled on). The ornate roofline includes dormers, gables, and chimneys. The house was donated in 1947 to the Jewish Museum. **1908**, *C. P. H. Gilbert.* **UES**

Gainsborough Studios
222 Central Park South
The studios here have great light and were evidently for wealthy artists. **1908**, *C. W. Buckham; frieze, Isidore Konti.* **MID**

Coty Building
714 Fifth Avenue
The stunning René Lalique windows are on a six-story building now housing Henri Bendel. **1908**, *Woodruff Leeming.* **MID**

Apthorp
2201 Broadway
● The monumental entrance to the twelve-story Apthorp leads to a landscaped courtyard with a carriage turnaround. It was built for William Waldorf Astor and occupies an entire city block. **1908**, *Clinton & Russell.* **UWS**

Franklin D. Roosevelt House
47-49 East 65th Street
Franklin Delano Roosevelt received this house as a wedding present from his mother, Sara. He convalesced here from polio between 1920 and 1922, but he spent little time here after he was elected governor in 1928 and president in 1932. The house was purchased for Hunter College in 1942. **1908**, *Charles A. Platt.* **UES**

the first flight
over New
York City, six
years after
Kitty Hawk.

Battery Maritime Building
11 South Street
● The steel Battery Maritime Building is elaborately decorated and painted green to imitate weathered copper. It was a terminal for Brooklyn ferries until 1938. Now it's used for Governors Island service. **1909**, *Walker & Morris*. FIN

The Police Building
240 Centre Street
● For nearly sixty-five years this building served as NYC police headquarters. The copper dome was restored by the same French artisans brought here to restore the Statue of Liberty. In 1973 the Police Department moved to One Police Plaza. In 1987 this Renaissance Revival building was converted to fifty-five condominiums. **1909**, *Hoppin, Koen and Huntington*. CIV

New York School of Applied Design for Women ▲
160 Lexington Avenue
Founded in 1892 to give women skills for the workplace, the progressive design school was housed in this Neoclassical building. The school later merged with the Pratt Institute. The frieze (top, detail) wrapping around the building is a small-scale reproduction of the frieze on the Parthenon. **1909**, Pell & Corbett. MID

Alwyn Court Apartments
182 West 58th Street
● Nearly all of this twelve-story facade is covered with rich French Renaissance-style ornament made of terra cotta. The apartment house, built with fourteen-room apartments, was subdivided during the Depression. **1909**, *Herbert S. Harde & R. Thomas Short*. MID

1910: The population of Manhattan is 2,331,542; Greater New York's is 4,766,883.
1910: Mayor William J. Gaynor is shot by a dismissed city official.
1910: Water is chlorinated in the city for the first time.
1910: The first ticker tape parade is held in Theodore Roosevelt's honor.

Surrogate's Court/Hall of Records ▲
31 Chambers Street

● Civic monuments were still meant to impress citizens — even when the building is designed merely for record storage. The white marble structure has cornice figures (top, detail) of notable New Yorkers, including Peter Stuyvesant. **1911**, *John R. Thomas; after Thomas' death in 1901 Horgan & Slattery completed the building; sculptor, Philip Martiny* CIV

Metropolitan Life Insurance Company ▲
1 Madison Avenue

● The fifty-four story marble tower was modeled after the Venetian campanile in the Piazza San Marco. The tower was decorated with two-hundred lion heads, ornamental columns, and a copper roof before it was drastically altered in 1961. It is topped with a gilded lantern (top) that flashes red on the quarter hour and red and white on the hour. The clock's minute hand is seventeen feet long and weighs a half-ton. At seven-hundred feet, the tower was the tallest building in NYC until 1913. *Building 1893; tower* **1909**, *both by Napoleon LeBrun & Sons.* FLT

Maurice Schinasi House
351 Riverside Drive

Schinasi made his fortune in tobacco processing and built this unattached, French Renaissance house. **1909**, *William B. Tuthill.* UWS

1911: There are ten Vanderbilt mansions on Fifth Avenue between 57th and 86th streets. **1911: Houses** are where 90 percent of "society" lives. In just twenty-five years, 90 percent of "society" will live in apartments. **1911: The Triangle Shirtwaist Fire** takes 145 lives, mostly women employees. The worst factory disaster in the city, it prompts the enforcement of fire safety regulations, and fire escapes proliferate across NYC.

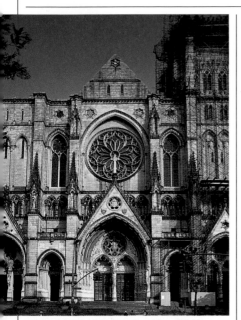

Cathedral of St. John the Divine ▲
Amsterdam Avenue at West 112th Street

● Great cathedrals took generations to build in medieval Europe. Some things don't change. This block-long cathedral was begun in 1892 in the Byzantine style. After partial construction, the design was modified in 1911 to reflect the new French Gothic fashion. Work was discontinued in 1941 and not resumed until the 1980s. A number of apprentices, under a master mason from England, work in the adjoining stone yard, learning skills that are all but lost in the United States. The angel with the trumpet positioned on the roof (above) is Gabriel. Considered the clearest messenger from earth to God, he is a common figure on churches. The cathedral has a seating capacity of about five thousand and room for thousands of standees. 1892-**1911**, *Heins & La Farge; 1911-1941, Cram & Ferguson.* HAR

First Precinct Station House
100 Old Slip

● This was the home of the 1st Precinct until 1973. In 1993 the Italian Renaissance-style palazzo became the home of the Landmarks Preservation Commission. **1911**, *Richard Howland Hunt & Joseph Howland Hunt.* FIN

The Peking
South Street Seaport

The 321-foot four-masted bark is similar to commercial ships in New York Harbor at the turn of the century. **1911**. FIN

1912: The *Titanic,* **bound for New York City's Chelsea Piers, sinks on its maiden** voyage to America, and 1,513 people die.
1913: The first federal

New York Public Library ▲
476 Fifth Avenue
● One of New York's best Beaux Arts buildings, the library was important enough to be opened by President William Howard Taft. The legacies of John Jacob Astor, James Lenox, and Samuel Tilden brought the library into being. Including the area under Bryant Park, the library holds up to ninety-two miles of books. The main reading room on the third floor seats 768 readers. The lions, *Patience* and *Fortitude* (top, detail), are by E. C. Potter. Above the main entrance Paul Wayland Bartlett's six

sculpted eleven-foot-high figures include *Poetry,* with a book, and *Drama,* holding two masks (above). Until 1899 the Croton Reservoir (see 1842) was on this site. **1911**, *John M. Carrère and Thomas Hastings.* MID

Croisic Building
220 Fifth Avenue
Overlooking Madison Square, this highly decorated, twenty-story office building is exhilarating. **1912**, *Frederick C. Browne.* FLT

Audubon Ballroom
165th Street and Broadway
Featuring opulent terra-cotta work, the facade is all that is left of what was once a movie and vaudville theater, and a ballroom. In 1965, the Black Muslim leader Malcolm X was assassinated at a rally here. The building was gutted in 1993 and Columbia University built the Audubon Science and Technology Park. **1912**, *Thomas W. Lamb.* HAR

income tax is levied in peacetime. **1913: Opium dens** are legal and prevalent in New York's Chinatown. The standard charge to visit one is two dollars.

Emigrant Industrial Savings Bank
51 Chambers Street
● This bank was established in 1851 for Irish immigrants. It's the third Emigrant building on the site. The seventeen-story building now houses municipal offices, including the Parking Violations Bureau. **1912**, *Raymond F. Almirall.* FIN

U.S. General Post Office
421 Eighth Avenue
● The inscription in the frieze, running along the two-block building, reads: "Neither snow nor rain nor heat nor gloom of night stays these couriers from the swift completion of their appointed rounds." It was adapted by the architect from the Eighth Book of Herodotus' Histories and has since become the motto of the Post Service. This many-columned building echoes McKim, Mead & White's Neoclassical Pennsylvania Station, once across the street (see 1965). **1913**, *McKim, Mead & White.* MID

Grand Central Terminal ▲
42nd Street and Park Avenue
● The terminal, the second on the site, was financed by Cornelius Vanderbilt's New York Central Railroad. The southern facade of this Beaux Arts structure is dominated by a thirteen-foot clock (top) and a large sculpture of Mercury, the god of commerce, Hercules, Minerva, and an

eagle. Inside, the plaster vaulted ceiling is decorated with a zodiac representing the winter sky painted backwards. The artist insisted that he painted it that way to allow people to picture the constellations the way God would see them! The gigantic windows have nine levels of catwalks, which can still be explored. **1913**, *Reed & Stem and Warren & Wetmore; sculptor, Jules Coutan.* MID

Carl Schurz
116th Street and Morningside Drive
Civic leaders were still revered in 1913, as shown by this Beaux Arts-style sculpture. Schurz was one of the most notable German immigrants in the 19th century: a brigadier general in the Civil War who became a journalist and powerful orator for civil rights. In 1911 the park running from 81st to 90th Street at the East River was named in his honor. **1913**, *Karl Bitter.* HAR

Woolworth Building ▲
233 Broadway

● Built, and paid for in cash, by Frank Woolworth, this was the headquarters of his chain of five-and-dime stores. The 792-foot graceful skyscraper—clad in creamy glazed terra cotta, Gothic tracery, and gargoyles—was the tallest building in the world until the Chrysler Building was completed (see 1930). It was the second-tallest structure in the world next to the Eiffel Tower at 1,045 feet. The marble lobby features a dazzling glass mosaic ceiling. The Woolworth Company still owns and operates the building. **1913**, *Cass Gilbert*. CIV

The New York Times Building
229 West 43rd Street

When the New York Times tower on Times Square became too cramped, this building was constructed to house both the editorial staff and the printing presses. **1913**, *Buchman & Fox; 1945 renovation, Shreve, Lamb & Harmon*. MID

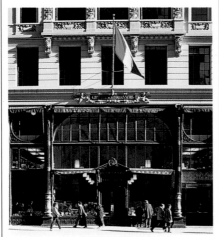

Charles Scribner's Sons
597 Fifth Avenue

● Scribner's Bookstore built this ten-story building and moved here from its lower Fifth Avenue offices. On the fourth floor are medallions of great printers, including Benjamin Franklin. Some great New York writers published by Scribner's include Edith Wharton and Henry James. **1913**, *Ernest Flagg*.

Church of the Intercession
540 West 155th Street

● The Gothic Revival church and cloister are set in the uptown Trinity Cemetery, the largest cemetery in Manhattan. These burial grounds opened in 1843, when the downtown Trinity Cemetery (see 1681) became too crowded. **1914**, *Cram, Goodhue & Ferguson*. HAR

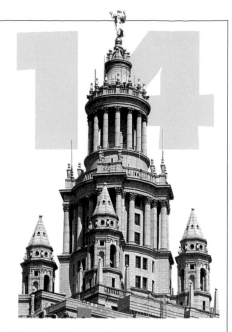

Municipal Building ▲
1 Centre Street

● These wedding cake-style towers cap off the Neoclassical skyscraper that straddles Chambers Street and houses civic offices. The towers, one symbolically for each borough, are surmounted by Adolph Weinman's twenty-five-foot gilt statue *Civic Fame*. **1914**, *McKim, Mead & White's first skyscraper.* CIV

Frick Collection
1 East 70th Street

● Built as the residence for Henry Clay Frick, the rags-to-riches chairman of the Carnegie Steel Corporation, with the intention of it one day becoming a small museum. Frick died in 1919, leaving $30 million worth of art. After Frick's widow died in 1931, the house was converted into a museum. The exterior is elegantly understated. **1914**, *Carrère and Hastings.* UES

The Knickerbocker Club
2 East 62nd Street

● This elegant Federal Revival building is the third home of the Knickerbocker Club, organized in 1871 by eighteen men who had become concerned about the lack of exclusivity at the Union Club. **1914**, *Delano & Aldrich.* UES

Mayor John P. Mitchel
Fifth Avenue at 90th Street

In office from **1914** to 1917 Mitchel was the youngest and one of the most able mayors in New York history. Not elected to a second term, he enlisted for duty in the Aviation Corps and was killed in training. *1926, Adolph A. Weinman.* CPK

Cliff Dweller's Apartments
243 Riverside Drive

Great friezes done in a western motif, including the buffalo skull above, appear on this apartment building. **1914**, *Herman Lee Meader.* HAR

1914

1915: A new city seal and official flag are adopted on the occasion of the 250th anniversary of the first mayor. They are designed by Paul Manship. 1915: The first transcontinental telephone line, from New York to San Francisco, is opened for commercial use. **1915: A subway accident** on the IRT takes 2 lives and injures 172 people.

1916: The first zoning ordinance in the United States is passed in NYC. It regulates building heights as a percentage of the lot to be covered. Setbacks become widespread. **1916: A trolley strike** shuts down most NYC lines for nearly six months. **1916: Union members** make up nearly one third of the city's workers. **1917: Motor**

Serge Sabarsky Foundation
1048 Fifth Avenue
Built for William Starr Miller and purchased in 1944 by Mrs. Cornelius Vanderbilt. The Sabarsky Foundation bought the house in 1994 to house an art museum. **1914**, *Carrère and Hastings.* UES

International Center of Photography
1130 Fifth Avenue
● This home was built for the diplomat and financier Willard D. Straight. The Straights founded the magazine *New Republic* here. The building was purchased in 1953 by the Audubon Society and in 1974 by the International Center of Photography. **1915**, *Delano & Aldrich.* UES

Yale Club
50 Vanderbilt Avenue
● At twenty-one stories, this Italian Renaissance-style building is the world's largest clubhouse, with perhaps the world's smallest sign — in one-inch-high letters. **1915**, *James Gamble Rodgers.* MID

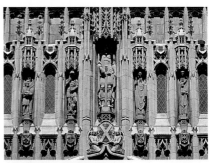

St. Thomas Church
1 West 53rd Street
● The St. Thomas congregation moved here from Houston Street in 1866. The first church on the site was destroyed by fire in 1905. The construction of the existing church was delayed when the congregation voted to send all the funds raised for rebuilding to the victims of the 1906 earthquake in San Francisco. Above the main entry is a beautiful reredos. **1916**, *Cram, Goodhue & Ferguson.* MID

vehicles are more prevalent than horses on the streets of the city.
1917: The Women Suffrage Amendment to the New York State Constitution is ratified.

1917: War is declared on Germany by Congress in April. During the war 1,656,000 American soldiers sail from New York to Europe.
1917: A steel net is submerged across the Narrows to prevent enemy submarines from entering the Upper Bay.

1918: Spanish influenza strikes, killing 12,500 in New York City and 500,000 in the United States.
1918: Horse-cars are virtually nonexistent.
1918: World War I ends.

New York Society Library
53 East 79th Street

Founded in 1754, this is the oldest library in the city. The private library began downtown on the current site of Federal Hall and then followed its readers north until it arrived here in 1937. Early users of the library included George Washington and Alexander Hamilton. The Italianate town house was built for John S. Rogers. **1917**, *Trowbridge & Livingston*. UES

Racquet and Tennis Club ▲
370 Park Avenue

The men's club, which was organized in 1875 as an athletic and social club, is housed in this muscular Florentine-style palazzo. It has New York's only court tennis court, the medieval precursor to modern tennis. Note the racket design (top) worked into the frieze under the cornice. **1918**, *McKim, Mead & White.* MID

George F. Baker Residence
76 East 93rd Street

● Built of brick and marble by the financier Francis F. Palmer. Purchased and extended by the banker George Baker in 1927. In 1958 the Synod of the Bishops of the Russian Orthodox Church outside of Russia purchased the house. **1918**, *Delano & Aldrich.* UES

Hotel des Artistes
1 West 67th Street

Built by a group of ten artists, the amusing neo-Gothic figures on the facade represent painters, writers, and musicians. The building has a history of well-known tenants. **1918**, *George Mort Pollard.* UWS

1919: General John J. Pershing leads a victory

parade up Fifth Avenue.
1920: The population of Manhattan is 2,284,103; Greater New York's is 5,620,048.
1920: Women can now vote nationally.

1920: Edith Wharton's *Age of Innocence*— a portrayal of

New York society in the 1870s—is published.
1920: Prohibition (Volstead Act) goes into effect for thirteen years. Thousands of speakeasies

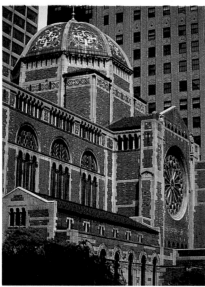

St. Bartholomew's Church ▲
109 East 50th Street

● The Byzantine-style church was built on the site of the Schaefer Brewing Company. Its Romanesque portal (below), designed by Stanford White in 1902, was preserved from the old St. Bartholomew's Church at Madison Avenue and 24th Street. The three knives (top) in the pediment are emblematic of St. Bartholomew, the saint that was flayed. He is the patron saint of tanners. **1919**, *Bertram G. Goodhue.* MID

Cunard Building ▲
25 Broadway

Originally a ticket office for ocean voyages, the American Renaissance building, with a striking interior, is currently operating as a post office branch. The exterior figures (one above) represent the four winds. **1921**, *Benjamin Wistar Morris.* FIN

Standard Oil Building
26 Broadway

The building configuration is the result of the Neoclassical style, complete with obelisks and urns, meeting the setback law (see 1916). The object at the top of the roof looks appropriately like an oil lamp. The first push-button elevator was installed here, making the elevator operator obsolete. **1922**, *Carrère and Hastings.* FIN

spring up in
the city.
**1920: A horse-
drawn
covered
wagon
explodes**
mysteriously
at Wall and
Nassau
Streets, killing
35 people and

injuring 130.
**1920: The first
radio station** is
established.
**1923: The
Yankees** move
from the Polo
Grounds at
155th Street to
their new
stadium in the
Bronx.

Bowery Savings Bank
110 East 42nd Street
The magnificent arched entry of this
bank has columns carved with images of
thrift, including misers and squirrels. In
1993 the Bowery Savings Bank became
Home Savings of America.**1923**, *York &
Sawyer*. MID

Bell Telephone Company Building
195 Broadway
The facade is composed of eight tiers of
Ionic columns. The panels above each
of the entrances representing the four
elements—earth, water, air, and fire
(above)—are by Paul Manship. **1924**,
William Welles Bosworth. FIN

American Radiator Building ▲
40 West 40th Street
● The dramatic coal-black brick and
glowing gold terra cotta reflect the
company's products: furnaces and
heaters. The Gothic-inspired Art Deco
spire is a classic. **1924**, *Raymond Hood
& Fouilhoux*. MID

The American Piano Company
Building
27 West 57th Street
The American Piano Company was so
proud of an award they had received,
they featured it prominently on their
building. **1924**, *Cross & Cross*. MID

The Colony Club
564 Park Avenue
The neo-Georgian building is the second
home of the Colony Club (see 1905).
1924, *Delano & Aldrich*. UES

1925: *The New Yorker* magazine is founded.
1925: John Dos Passos's

novel *Manhattan Transfer*, depicting NYC life in the 1920s, is published.

1927: The Holland Tunnel to New Jersey is opened. Its named after it's chief engineer,

Clifford M. Holland.
1927: Charles A. Lindbergh flies nonstop and solo from

Federal Reserve Bank
33 Liberty Street
● Fourteen stories aboveground and five below, this Florentine palazzo-style building is one of twelve Federal Reserve Banks in the United States. Each note issued through this branch has a *B* on it. **1924**, *York & Sawyer.* FIN

Independence Flagstaff
Union Square
This flagstaff base is thirty-six feet in diameter and eight feet high and covered with bronze reliefs representing the evolution of democracy. It was erected on the 150th anniversary of the Declaration of Independence. **1926**, *sculptor, Anthony De Francisci.* FLT

City Center
135 West 55th Street
● Built in the Moorish style to be an entertainment hall for the New York Shriners, NYC acquired the building in 1942 and made it the home of the New York City Ballet and the New York City Opera. **1924**, *Harry P.Knowles.* MID

Mayor Jimmy Walker's Residence
6 St. Luke's Place
A classic Federal-style row house (center) was the home of Jimmy Walker, mayor from **1926** to 1932. His flamboyant style was well suited to the 1920s. Two lanterns customarily distinguished a mayor's residence. 1850s, *unknown architect.* GRV

The Con Edison Building
4 Irving Place
The Con Ed tower is one of the few NYC skyscrapers lit to reflect the changing seasons and holidays. 1915-29, *Henry J. Hardenbergh; the unique tower,* **1926**, *Warren & Wetmore.* FLT

Graybar Building
420 Lexington Avenue
The bronze cones (representing devices placed on ship's lines to prevent rats from climbing on board) and rats on the canopy symbolized the twenty-six-floor building's anchorage in the midst of the country's greatest maritime city. **1926**, *Sloan & Robertson.* MID

Sherry-Netherland Hotel ▲
59th Street and Fifth Avenue
The thirty-eight-story building was the world's tallest apartment hotel when it was completed. **1927**, *Schultze & Weaver.* MID

Paramount Building
1501 Broadway
● The thirty-three-story Neoclassical Paramount Building sports a distinctive Art Deco top. **1927**, *Rapp & Rapp.* MID

Tudor City
Tudor City Place
A complex of twelve buildings, Tudor City was designed in the American Tudor style. It includes three thousand apartments, shops, and gardens. To avoid looking over what were slaughterhouses and slums, the building sides facing east are nearly windowless. **1927**, *Fred F. French Co., H. Douglas Ives.* MID

1928: Al Smith, born on the Lower East Side and governor of New York, runs unsuccessfully for the presidency against Herbert Hoover. **1928: There are more autos in NYC than in all of Europe. 1929: Robert Moses** opens Jones Beach State Park. With public transportation, parkways, bridges, and tunnels he makes areas beyond the city more accessible for the middle

Pythian Temple ▲
135 West 70th Street
Buildings with Egyptian Revival-style details were popularized by the discovery of King Tut's tomb in 1922. **1927**, *Thomas W. Lamb.* UWS

Cornelius Vanderbilt Gates
Fifth Avenue at 105th Street
When Cornelius Vanderbilt's 1880 home at Fifth Avenue and 59th Street was torn down in **1927**, the gates were salvaged. In 1939 they were installed at the 105th Street entrance to the Conservatory Garden (see 1936) in Central Park. *1884, Bergrotte and Bauviller.* CPK

Central Savings Bank
2100 Broadway
● Whimsical ironwork embellishes the imposing bank facade. Established in 1859, it was called the German Savings Bank until World War I, when anti-German sentiment arose. **1928**, *York & Sawyer; ironwork, Samuel Yellin.* UWS

New York State Supreme Court
60 Centre Street
Behind the portico the New York County Courthouse building is hexagonal. **1927**, *Guy Lowell.* GRV

Hearst Magazine Building
959 Eighth Avenue
Commissioned by William Randolph Hearst, the stubby six-story building looks incomplete, as is the case. It was meant to be a skyscraper, but funds ran out. Pairs of sculptures resting at the base of the columns include *Comedy and Tragedy* by Henry Kreis. **1928**, *Joseph Urban.* MID

class to live or just visit.
1929: The stock market collapses on October 29, launching the Depression. Most skyscrapers under construction were completed, but virtually no new ones were begun again until the late 1940s.

New York Life Insurance Company ▲
51 Madison Avenue
Built on the site of the first Madison Square Garden, this thirty-four-story building features one of the architect's signature pyramidal crowns. The Gothic ornament is delightful (detail, top). **1928**, *Cass Gilbert.* FLT

Chanin Building ▲
122 East 42nd Street
● The Art Deco fifty-six-story skyscraper has an ornamental base (detail, top) and is wrapped with a striking bronze frieze illustrating the theory of evolution, starting with marine life (detail, above). Built for the developer Irwin Chanin. **1929**, *Sloan & Robertson.* MID

Temple Emanu-El
1 East 65th Street
One of the largest synagogues in the world, the temple seats twenty-five hundred people — more than St. Patrick's Cathedral. **1929**, *Robert O. Kohn, Charles Butler and Clarence Stein.* UES

New York Central Building
230 Park Avenue
Built for offices of the railroads using Grand Central, this was later called the New York General Building. With its decorative cupola, portals for traffic, and large clock, it was a focal point for miles north and south on Park Avenue until the Pan Am Building went up in 1963. In 1977 it became the Helmsley Building. **1929**, *Warren & Wetmore.* MID

In 1928 **York Avenue** was named for Sergeant Alvin York, a quiet soldier who earned the Medal of Honor and nearly fifty other decorations during World War I, becoming the nation's hero.

I. Miller Building ▲
1552 Broadway
I. Miller, owner of a shoe store frequented by theatrical people, commissioned life-size sculptures of four popular actresses for his store's building. **1929**, *sculptor, Alexander Stirling Calder.* MID

San Remo Apartments
145 Central Park West
● Capping the San Remo, these towers were designed to conceal water tanks. Styled after a Roman temple, they are clearly visible from the far side of Central Park. **1930**, *Emery Roth.* UWS

40 Wall Street
Fortunately the top of this building is interesting because it has a significant presence on the downtown skyline. **1929**, *H. Craig Severance and Yasuo Matsui.* FIN

Fuller Building
45 East 57th Street
● The original Fuller Building was the Flatiron Building (see 1902). This elegant Art Deco building features an entrance clock with sculpted figures by Elie Nadelman. **1929**, *Walker & Gillette.* MID

Loew's Theater
175th Street at Broadway
This flamboyant movie theater, coated with decorative terra cotta, would look at home in Los Angeles. **1930**, *Thomas W. Lamb.* HAR

Chrysler Building
405 Lexington Avenue

● The Chrysler Automobile Company built this 1,046-foot Art Deco skyscraper, the tallest building in the world until the Empire State Building went up eighteen months later in 1931. The stainless steel and white ceramic-brick exterior is decorated with automotive imagery, including gargoyles fashioned after hood ornaments. **1930**, *William Van Alen.* MID

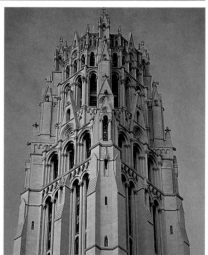

Riverside Church
121st Street and Riverside Drive

The 392-foot Gothic tower houses world's largest bell, but is mostly church offices *disguised* as a bell tower. The church was a gift of John D. Rockefeller. **1930**, *Allen & Collens and Henry C. Pelton.* HAR

Daily News Building
220 East 42nd Street

The *Daily News*, the first successful tabloid in the United States, was housed here. Established in 1919, it had become New York's best-selling paper by 1925. The *News* sold the building in 1982 and no longer occupies it. This building was featured in *Superman* movies as the home of the *Daily Planet.* **1930**, *John Mead Howells & Raymond Hood.* MID

George Washington Bridge
West 181st Street at the Hudson River

The George Washington Bridge was the world's longest suspension bridge — 3,500 feet — until the Golden Gate Bridge opened in San Francisco. It's the only NYC bridge spanning the Hudson River. **1931**, *engineer, O. H. Ammann; Cass Gilbert, Inc.* HAR

Empire State Building
350 Fifth Avenue
The Empire State Building was the world's tallest building until the World Trade towers were built in 1973. It is 1,250 feet to the top of the unused dirigible mooring mast. The speculative office building opened during the depression and was called the Empty State Building for a number of years. In 1945 a B-25 bomber, lost in a fog, hit the seventy-ninth floor, killing fourteen people. The limestone, granite, and aluminum structure is featured in a number of movies from *King Kong* to *Sleepless in Seattle*. The top floors were first floodlit when the Yankees won the World Series in 1977. **1931**, *Shreve, Lamb & Harmon.* MID

General Electric Building ▲
570 Lexington Avenue
● The imagery on this fifty-story Art Deco building includes electric bolts and mechanical faces; it reflects the business of its builder, RCA, the Radio Corporation of America. General Electric (detail, top) owned the building until the 1990s when it donated it to Columbia University. **1931**, *Cross & Cross.* MID

McGraw-Hill Building
330 West 42nd Street
An International-style building with Art Deco detailing that looks as if it's in need of some repair. Currently owned by Group Health Insurance. **1931**, *Raymond Hood, Godley & Fouilhoux.* MID

The Waldorf-Astoria
301 Park Avenue
● The hotel was built in the Art Deco style, then remodeled in the sixties. The original style is still visible in some details and the towers. Herbert Hoover lived here from 1934 until his death in 1964. **1931**, *Schultze & Weaver.* MID

Walker resigns as mayor and goes to Europe for three years, after a municipal corruption investigation gets under way. **1933:**

Prohibition is repealed. **1933: Three super piers** are built on the Hudson River between 48th and 52nd streets to handle the

huge new passenger ships. **1934: The first sales tax** is imposed by La Guardia, 2 percent for unemployment relief.

Mayor Fiorello La Guardia △
La Guardia Place
La Guardia was elected mayor in **1933** and held office for three terms. He's fondly remembered for reading the comics on the radio during a newspaper strike. This statue exudes energy and is not far from Sullivan Street, where he was born. *Unveiled in 1994, Neil Estern.* GRV

Union League Club
38 East 37th Street
The club was founded in 1863 by Republicans who left the Union Club in protest over its failure to oust Confederate sympathizers. **1931**, *Morris & O'Connor.* MID

Radio City Music Hall
1260 Avenue of the Americas
● Radio City was built as a variety house but soon became *the* place to open a film—over 650 features debuted here. In 1979 music spectaculars were introduced. The lobby is an extravagance of Art Deco detailing. **1932**, *chief designer Raymond Hood.* MID

Museum of the City of New York
1220 Fifth Avenue
● The neo-Georgian style, with its strong English references, was an interesting choice of style for the Museum of the City of New York. A life-size bronze of Alexander Hamilton (above) is set in a niche in the north wing of the museum. The MCNY annually commemorates the original sale of Manhattan with its "24-Dollar" award honoring a private citizen for service to NCY. Brendan Gill and Walter Cronkite are among the past recipients. **1932**, *Joseph H. Freedlander; sculptor, Adolph A. Weinman.* UES

Union Club
101 East 69th Street
This 18th-century English-style building houses the Union Club, the oldest social club in New York, founded in 1836, by ex-Mayor Philip Hone, among others. **1932**, *Delano & Aldrich.* UES

FROM 1934

1934: Robert Moses is named parks commissioner. The Parks Department starts to develop or remodel eight parks and seventy-nine playgrounds in Manhattan alone, adding 579 acres for recreation. **1930s: The FDR Drive** is begun and built on landfill. Some of the later landfill comes from the ballast of ships from England; it's the rubble of buildings

The Apollo Theater ▲
235 West 125th Street
The vaudeville shows in Hurtig and Seaman's New Theater appealed to the middle-class white Harlem audience. The racial mix of the neighborhood changed, and in **1934** the theater came into the limelight as the Apollo, a popular showcase for black entertainers, including Billie Holiday and Duke Ellington. *1914, George Keister.* HAR

New York Hospital
York Avenue from 68th to 70th Streets
A massive medical complex extending to the East River. **1933**, *Coolidge, Shepley, Bulfinch and Abbott.* UES

Three Dancing Maidens
Conservatory Gardens, Central Park
The fountain sculpture, a gift of the Samuel Untermyer family, was installed in 1947. *Circa 1910, sculptor, Walter Schott;* **1936**, *landscape by M. Betty Sprout.* CPK

Rockefeller Center ▲
● The original complex consisted of thirteen buildings on twelve acres and employed 75,000 men over ten years of construction. Over two-hundred small buildings, mostly tenements, were leveled for Rockefeller Center. The complex, now eighteen buildings on twenty-one acres, works successfully as a city within a city. The simple limestone buildings are set off by over one hundred Art Deco murals and sculptures, each with a "humanistic" theme. The soaring RCA Building (top) is set in the middle of the center. Paul Manship's *Prometheus* (above) is the focal point of the central plaza. The winged *Mercury* by Lee Lawrie is another one of the many art works (detail, below). **1934**, *Chief designer Raymond Hood.* MID

destroyed
during the blitz.
**1936:
Television** is
first broadcast.
**1936: The
hottest day**
ever recorded
in NYC is 102.3°
in the shade.
**1937: The
Lincoln Tunnel**
opens.

1937: Women
can now serve
on juries.
**1939: La
Guardia Airport**
opens.
**1940: The
population** of
Manhattan is
1,889,924;
Greater New
York's is
7,454,995.

U.S. Courthouse ▲
40 Centre Street

● This is one of the last Neoclassical commercial buildings put up in New York. It is thirty-one stories and capped with a gold pyramid. **1936**, *Cass Gilbert died in 1934; the work was completed by his son Cass Gilbert, Jr.* CIV

The Cloisters
Fort Tryon Park

Fort Tryon Park, over sixty acres, was purchased by John D. Rockefeller, who then financed the building of the museum on four acres of the park. Portions of five French medieval monasteries were incorporated into this museum devoted to medieval art. It is now part of the Metropolitan Museum. **1938**, *Allen, Collens & Willis.* UPM

Tiffany & Company ▲
727 Fifth Avenue

Tiffany's is an austere building with this nine-foot-high wooden figure of Atlas (top) above its entry. The figure was brought from the jeweler's previous location—Fifth Avenue and 37th Street, as it had been from the site before that one—Union Square West. **1940**, *Cross & Cross.* MID

Museum of Modern Art
11 West 53rd Street

Innovative at the time, MOMA was built in the International style. The museum's strength is art from the first half of this century, including impressionists, cubists, and realists. The sculpture garden (below), part of a later addition by Philip Johnson, is one of the city's most pleasant outdoor spaces. **1939**, *Philip L. Goodwin and Edward Durell Stone.* MID

1941

1941: Pearl Harbor is bombed by Japan, bringing the United States into the war. Nearly 900,000 New Yorkers go into the armed forces; 16,106 do not return.

1941: Most construction halts during the war. Skyscrapers are blacked out until the war ends.

1942: The *Normandie*, while being outfitted for war, catches fire and capsizes at its dock on the Hudson River.

1948: A one-billion-dollar municipal budget, a NYC first, is announced.

1948: The

Tammany Hall ▲
Union Square at 17th Street
Symbolically marking the end of Tammany's influence (see 1789), this building, the last Tammany Hall in NYC, was sold in **1943**. Note the fraternal Tammany red cap in the pediment (detail, top). It now houses a theater.
1929, unknown architect. FLT

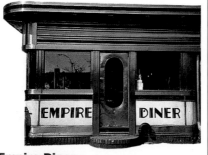

Empire Diner
210 Tenth Avenue
The classic American stainless steel diner is alive and well. **1943**, *original architect unknown; remodeled in 1976, Carl Laanes.* CHE

Chaplain's Memorial
Riverside Drive and 121st Street
Easily overlooked in the grass across from Riverside Church, this bronze plaque honors four chaplains, "who, after giving their life belts to their fellow servicemen, locked arms and praying, went down together with the transport *Dorchester* sunk by a German submarine February 3, **1943**." HAR

Municipal Asphalt Plant
655 East 90th Street
● In this unique concrete building asphalt was produced for NYC streets. In 1982 it was converted to a recreational area. **1944**, *Kahn & Jacobs.* UWS

In1945, in the course of lobbying for NYC to become the home of the United Nations, Mayor Fiorello La Guardia renamed Sixth Avenue the **Avenue of the Americas**.

transit fare, five cents since 1904, is raised to ten cents.
1949: E. B. White's *Here Is New York* is published.
1950: The population of Manhattan is 1,960,101; Greater New York's is 7,891,957—five hundred times the density of the national average.
1950: Alger Hiss, allegedly a spy, is tried and convicted of perjury in New York City.
1950: Mayor William O'Dwyer leaves office midterm amid rumors of corruption.
1950: Senator Joseph McCarthy charges that Communists have infiltrated the State Department.

Stuyvesant Town
14th to 20th Street, East of First Avenue
Stuyvesant Town was middle-income housing built for returning World War II veterans by the Metropolitan Life Insurance Company (see 1909). Fountains and gardens are interspersed among thirteen- and fourteen-story brick apartment blocks. **1947**, *Irwin Clavan and Gilmore Clarke.* LES

The Carousel
Central Park
A merry-go-round has been in Central Park since 1871. The original was powered by real horses that walked a treadmill in an underground pit. This one, featuring hand-carved horses, was built in 1903 at Coney Island and moved to its current location in **1951**. CPK

The United Nations
First Avenue and 42nd to 48th Street
The United Nations, with its own police force and post office, is technically outside the jurisdiction of the United States. The three-building complex is set in seventeen acres donated by John D. Rockefeller, Jr. The main buildings were designed by an international committee of twelve architects, including Le Corbusier, under the chairmanship of Wallace K. Harrison. The thirty-nine-story Secretariat Building was completed in 1950; the Conference Building and General Assembly (above) opened two years later. **1952**, *a consortium chaired by Wallace K. Harrison.* MID

1953: Convicted of spying, New Yorkers Ethel and Julius Rosenberg are sent to the electric chair. 1954: Robert F. Wagner begins his three terms as mayor. 1955: The last Manhattan el, on Third Avenue, is dismantled. 1956: The Bard Law is passed. For the first time historic, cultural, and aesthetic considerations are taken into account in determining zoning. 1957: *West Side Story,* the musical by Leonard Bernstein opens. 1957: Racial discrimination is made illegal by the Fair Housing Law. 1959: NYC considers statehood for itself, because it is unhappy with its legislature representation. 1960: The population of Manhattan is 1,698,281; Greater New York's is 7,781,984. Manhattan's population declines for the first time since 1930. 1963: The

Lever House
390 Park Avenue
Lever House was the first of Park Avenue's glass- and steel-fronted buildings. It also initiated the use of a pedestrian plaza. The turquoise panels, characteristic of the company's cleaning products, reflected the company's fresh and clean image. **1952**, *Skidmore, Owings & Merrill.* MID

The Seagram Building
375 Park Avenue
The exquisitely designed thirty-eight-story skyscraper was made with the finest materials. The city was so pleased with the plaza that the zoning laws were amended to offer incentives for other plazas and arcades. **1958**, *Ludwig Mies van der Rohe and Philip Johnson.* MID

Hans Christian Andersen
Central Park
The winsome sculpture of Andersen, author of *The Ugly Duckling,* continues to charm children. **1956**, *George Lober.* CPK

A wave of artists moved into the inexpensive lofts in the warehouses south of Houston Street. The acronym **SoHo**, "south of Houston," was coined in the 1960s.

In 1654 Asser Levy, the city's first kosher butcher, became a leading citizen after Governor Peter Stuyvesant tried unsuccessfully to discriminate against the Jewish Levy and bar him from serving in the militia. **Asser Levy Place** was named in 1954, upon the tercentenary of his arrival in New Amsterdam.

nation mourns the death of President John F. Kennedy. **1964: Rioting** breaks out in Harlem. **1965: A power failure** paralyzes NYC for thirteen hours. There is a minor "baby boom" nine months later. **1965:** **Pennsylvania Station** is torn down. The event is the catalyst for the city to establish the Landmarks Preservation Commission. **1966: A NYC income and commuter tax** is established.

East Coast Memorial
Battery Park
The large bronze eagle is set amid eighteen-foot granite blocks listing the 4,596 Americans who died in the Atlantic in World War II. The eagle clutches a funerary wreath, the symbol of victory over death. President John F. Kennedy unveiled the monument in **1963**. *Sculptor, Albino Manca.*

Chatham Towers
170 Park Row
These distinct towers made from cast concrete are public housing. **1965,** *Kelly & Gruzen.* LES

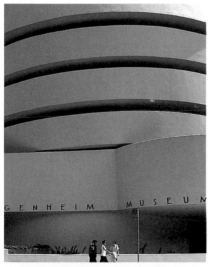

Solomon R. Guggenheim Museum
1071 Fifth Avenue
● Frank Lloyd Wright's only building in NYC is this extraordinary concrete structure. It was sixteen years in design and construction. The museum was established by the copper magnate Solomon Guggenheim for his nonobjective art collection. **1959,** *Frank Lloyd Wright; most recent addition, 1992, by Gwathmey Siegel & Associates Architects.* UES

Whitney Museum of American Art
Madison Avenue at 75th Street
The Whitney Museum looks like a foreboding granite fortress, but the interior functions well for the museum. It was founded in 1930 by Gertrude Vanderbilt Whitney. **1966,** *Marcel Breuer and Hamilton Smith.* UES

1967: The Singer Building is demolished. Built in 1908 and 612 feet tall, it is the highest building ever torn down.
1967: The

musical *Hair* opens in NYC.
1969: The astronauts walk on the moon.
1969: The World Series is won by the Mets.
1970: The population of

Manhattan declines again to 1,539,233; Greater New York's is 7,895,563, of which more than 1.4 million are foreign-born.
1970: The transit fare

rises to thirty cents.
1974: Richard M. Nixon resigns the presidency.
1974: The New York Passenger Ship Terminal is completed.

Lincoln Center
Columbus Avenue and 64th Street
● Lincoln Center is situated on fourteen acres. The three buildings facing the central plaza are Avery Fisher Hall, home of the New York Philharmonic; the Metropolitan Opera House (above), featuring two large murals by Marc Chagall; and the New York State Theater. The center was completed in **1968**. *Various architects with a master plan by Wallace K. Harrison.* **UWS**

Paley Plaza Park
3 East 53rd Street
The soothing waterfall is a backdrop on this forty-two-by one-hundred-foot plaza, a model for vest-pocket parks. The space, site of the original Stork Club, was donated to the city by William Paley. **1967**, *Zion & Breen.* **MID**

Ford Foundation Building
320 East 43rd Street
The structure is wrapped around a one-third-acre garden set in a 130-foot-high space. **1967**, *Kevin Roche, John Dinkeloo & Associates.* **MID**

Martin Luther King, Jr., Memorial
122 Amsterdam Avenue
The civil rights leader was assassinated in **1968**. The Martin Luther King, Jr., High School chose to remember him with this twenty-eight-foot uncoated steel cube, which changes continuously as it weathers. It stands in front of the school. 1975, *sculptor, William Tarr.* **UWS**

1975: Defaulting on its bonds and loans, NYC is temporarily bailed out by the federal government. **1975: The Vietnam War** ends.

1976: The U.S. Bicentennial is celebrated with a great harbor festival in NYC. **1977: A twenty-five-hour power outage** leads to widespread looting.

Group of Four Trees
Chase Manhattan Plaza
The forty-two-foot tall sculpture is a delightful contrast with the adjacent sixty-story Chase Manhattan Bank. **1972**, *sculptor, Jean Dubuffet*. FIN

Mount Morris Park, bisecting Fifth Avenue between 120th and 124th Streets, was renamed **Marcus Garvey Park** in 1973 in recognition of the black leader who tried to organize a back-to-Africa movement in the early 1920s. The area became a park only because the seventy-foot-high rocky hill in its midst was considered unsuitable for building lots. HAR

Roosevelt Island Tramway ▲
The aerial tramway crosses 250 feet above the East River in three-and-one-half minutes, connecting 60th Street in Manhattan with a residential development on Roosevelt Island (formerly Welfare Island). Traveling at 16 mph, the tramway provides wonderful views of the East Side. **1976**, *Prentice & Chan, Ohlhausen*. MID

World Trade Center
World Trade Plaza
These twin 110-story towers, flanked by five low buildings on a five-acre plaza, form a city within a city. They are the world's second-tallest building after the Sears Tower in Chicago. Over fifty thousand people are employed here. This was the site of a destructive terrorist bombing in February 1993: Six people were killed and nearly one thousand were injured. The towers were completed four years before the rest of the center. **1977**, *Minoru Yamasaki & Associates and Emery Roth & Sons*. FIN

The Rabbi Lookstein Upper School
60 East 78th Street
The school with the remarkable aluminum facade replaced five brownstones. **1980**, *Conklin & Rossant.* UES

Citicorp Center
153 East 53rd Street
The fifty-four-story aluminum-clad skyscraper rests on four piers and offers a five-story retail plaza. The great skyline silhouette is created by the angled top, designed to house a solar collector that was never installed. **1977**, *Hugh Stubbins & Associates.* MID

Trump Tower
725 Fifth Avenue
The residential and retail glass tower is popular with tourists. **1983**, *Der Scutt and Swanke Hayden Connell.* MID

Trompe l'Oeil
Peck Slip
The Brooklyn Bridge mural disguises a former Con Ed substation in the historic South Street district. **1979**, *artist Richard Haas.* FIN

transit fare goes up to 75 cents. **1983: Brooklyn Bridge Centennial** is celebrated. **1985: Edward** Koch is re-elected for his third term as mayor. **1986: The Statue of Liberty**'s 100th anniversary is celebrated.

IBM Building
590 Madison Avenue
The forty-three story black granite monolith is cantilevered over its own entrance. **1983**, *Edward Larrabee Barnes Associates.*MID

The AT&T Building
550 Madison Avenue
The granite Post Modern skyscraper that looks like a Chippendale highboy was built for AT&T. It is now the Sony Building. **1984**, *Philip Johnson/John Burgee.* MID

Evans View ▲
303 East 60th Street
Situated mid-block, this residential high-rise is wider than the forty-feet maximum to qualify as a sliver building. **1986**, *Gruzen Partners and Abe Rothenburg Associates.* UES

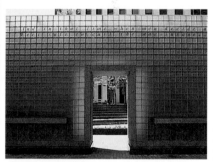

New York Vietnam Veterans Memorial
Vietnam Veterans Plaza
Here's a segment of a fourteen-foot-high, seventy-foot long glass-block wall etched with news and soldiers' letters written home. **1985**, *William Britt Fellows, Peter Wormser.* FIN

Jacob Javits Convention Center
655 West 34th Street
Spread over five-square blocks, this black crystal palace is one of the largest convention centers in the United States. It takes little advantage of its site overlooking the Hudson River. **1986**, *I. M. Pei and Partners.* MID .

1987: New York Stock Exchange seat sells for a record one-million dollars.

1987: The stock market plummets over 500 points in one day.

Lipstick Building
885 Third Avenue
The elliptical office building acquired its name for obvious reasons. The architect's rationale for the shape was to break up the wall of buildings lining the avenue. **1986**, *John Burgee with Philip Johnson.* MID

Financial Square
32 Old Slip
The four corners of the thirty-four-story skyscraper are angled and tapered upward offering more corner offices than conventional floorplans. **1987**, *Edward Durrell Stone and Associates.* FIN

Corinthian
645 First Avenue
This soaring residential tower is softened by the stacks of scalloped bay windows. **1987**, *Der Scutt and Michael Schimenti.* MID

17 State Street
The bowed glass surface is stunning when it reflects sunsets over the harbor. **1988**, *Emery Roth & Sons.* FIN
AT BATTERY PARK

1989: The Berlin Wall comes down.
1989: David N. Dinkins is elected mayor.

1989: B. Altman's closes it's doors after 124 years of business.

Winter Garden
2 World Financial Center
The barrel-vaulted palm-filled public space functions as a hub for the World Financial Center. **1988**, *Cesar Pelli and Adamson Associates.* FIN

Looking Toward the Avenue
1301 Avenue of the Americas
At fourteen and eighteen feet tall, these are two of the three *Venus de Milo* variations installed in front of Crédit Lyonnais. The classical reference is a good contrast with the austere skyscrapers. *Installed in* **1989**, *Jim Dine.* MID

Worldwide Plaza ▲
49th to 50th Street, Eighth to Ninth Avenue
The plaza is dominated by two towers. This one is an office tower; the second one is smaller and residential. **1989**, *Skidmore, Owings & Merrill; the residential tower, Frank Williams.* MID

Museum of Broadcasting
23 West 52nd Street
The museum was founded by William S. Paley and built on land he donated. **1989**, *John Burgee with Philip Johnson.* MID

Upper East Side Cultural Center
201 East 96th Street
This mosque is traditionally oriented toward Islam's Mecca. **1989**, *Skidmore, Owings & Merrill.* UES

Battery Park City

In 1971 the old piers were removed and in 1973 the landfilling began, much of it coming from the excavation of the World Trade tower's foundation. By 1980 the first buildings were completed. By **1990**, on the ninety-two acres of Battery Park City, there were 30 acres of park, housing for 7,000 people, a one-and-one-half mile promenade along the river, and a variety of sculpture including the one above by Tom Otterness. *1990, master plan by Cooper & Eckstut.* FIN

Mondrian
250 East 54th Street

The forty-three-story apartment building was named for its colorful banding after the Dutch cubist artist, Piet Mondrian, in a contest organized by the developers among realtors. **1991**, *Fox & Fowles.* MID

International Building
750 Lexington Avenue

The conical top gives the thirty-one story office building a distinctive profile. **1989,** *Helmut Jahn.* MID

World Financial Center
Battery Park City

Three of the four high-rise buildings are shown above. From left to right: The pyramid-topped building is American Express headquarters, 1986; the dome-topped one is Merrill Lynch's, 1988; the third building is headquarters for a number of companes including Dow Jones, 1986. The center was completed in the early **1990**s. *Cesar Pelli.* FIN

spoken by
New Yorkers.
Spanish is the
second most
common after

English.
**1991: NYC real
estate** is
valued at
$139,820

million.
**1994: NYC full-
time employees**
are estimated
to number

238,641.
**1994: Rudolf
Giuliani** is
inaugurated
mayor.

Trump Palace
200 East 69th Street
At fifty-five-stories this apartment
building is prominent on the Upper East
Side skyline. **1991**, *Frank Williams &
Associates.* UES

100 United Nations Plaza
East 48th Street
The striking silhouette of this fifty-five
story residential building is formed by
set backs on the top eight floors. The
triangular form is reiterated in the
balconies. **1992**, *Der Scutt.* MID

Tribeca Bridge
West Side Highway at Chambers Street
Without this bridge, accessible by both
stairs and elevator, Stuyvesant High
School could never have been built on
the far side of the busy West Side
Highway. **1992**, *Skidmore, Owings &
Merrill.* SOH

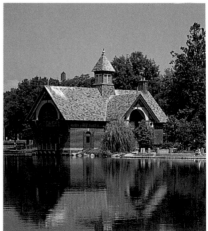

Dana Discovery Center
Harlem Meer, Central Park
Set on the bucolic-looking northern edge
of Central Park, this building serves as a
visitor's center and offers programs with
an educational and environmental thrust.
1993, *Buttrick White & Burtis.* CPK

NEW YORK FILE

NYC MAYORS

1665	Thomas Willett	1826	Philip Hone
1666	Thomas Delavall	1827	William Paulding
1667	Thomas Willett	1829	Walter Bowne
1668	Cornelius Steenwyck	1833	Gideon Lee
1671	Thomas Delavall	1834	Cornelius V. Lawrence
1672	Matthias Nicolls	1837	Aaron Clark
1673	John Lawrence	1839	Isaac L. Varian
1675	William Dervall	1841	Robert H. Morris
1676	Nicholas De Meyer	1844	James Harper
1677	Stephanus Van Cortlandt	1845	William F. Havemeyer
1678	Thomas Delavall	1846	Andrew H. Mickle
1679	Francis Rombouts	1847	William V. Brady
1680	William Dyre	1848	William F. Havemeyer
1682	Cornelius Steenwyck	1849	Caleb S. Woodhull
1684	Gabriel Minvielle	1851	Ambrose C. Kingsland
1685	Nicholas Bayard	1853	Jacob A. Westervelt
1686	Stephanus Van Cortlandt	1855	Fernando Wood
1689	Peter Delanoy	1858	Daniel F. Tiemann
1691	John Lawrence	1860	Fernando Wood
1692	Abraham De Peyster	1862	George Opdyke
1694	Charles Lodwick	1864	C. Godfrey Gunther
1695	William Merritt	1866	John T. Hoffman
1698	Johannes De Peyster	1868	Thomas Coman
1699	David Provoost	1869	A. Oakey Hall
1700	Isaac De Reimer	1873	William F. Havemeyer
1701	Thomas Noell	1874	S. B. H. Vance
1702	Philip French	1875	William H. Wickham
1703	William Peartree	1877	Smith Ely
1707	Ebenezer Wilson	1879	Edward Cooper
1710	Jacobus Van Cortlandt	1881	William R. Grace
1711	Caleb Heathcote	1883	Franklin Edson
1714	John Johnstone	1885	William R. Grace
1719	Jacobus Van Cortland	1887	Abram S. Hewitt
1720	Robert Walters	1888	Hugh J. Grant
1725	Johannes Jansen	1893	Thomas F. Gilroy
1726	Robert Lurting	1895	William L. Strong
1735	Paul Richard	1898	Robert A. Van Wyck
1739	John Cruger	1902	Seth Low
1744	Stephen Bayard	1904	George B. McClellan
1747	Edward Holland	1910	William J. Gaynor
1757	John Cruger, Jr.	1913	Ardolph L. Kline
1766	Whitehead Hicks	1914	John Purroy Mitchel
1776	David Matthews	1918	John F. Hylan
1784	James Duane	1926	James J. Walker
1789	Richard Varick	1932	Joseph V. McKee
1801	Edward Livingston	1933	John P. O'Brien
1803	De Witt Clinton	1934	Fiorello H. La Guardia
1807	Marinus Willett	1946	William O'Dwyer
1808	De Witt Clinton	1950	Vincent R. Impellitteri
1810	Jacob Radcliff	1954	Robert F. Wagner
1811	De Witt Clinton	1966	John V. Lindsey
1815	John Ferguson	1974	Abraham Beame
1816	Jacob Radcliffe	1978	Edward Koch
1818	Cadwallader D. Colden	1990	David Dinkins
1821	Stephen Allen	1994	Rudolph Giuliani
1825	William Paulding		

NEW YORK FILE

GOVERNORS

1777	George Clinton
1795	John Jay*
1801	George Clinton
1804	Morgan Lewis
1807	Daniel Tompkins
1817	John Taylor
1817	De Witt Clinton*
1823	Joseph Christopher Yates
1825	De Witt Clinton*
1828	Nathaniel Pitcher
1829	Martin Van Buren
1829	Enos Thompson Throop
1833	William Learned Marcy
1839	William H. Seward
1843	William C. Bouck
1845	Silas Wright
1847	John Young
1849	Hamilton Fish*
1851	Washington Hunt
1853	Horatio Seymour
1855	Myron Clark
1857	John Alsop King
1859	Edwin D. Morgan*
1863	Horatio Seymour
1865	Reuben Eaton Fenton
1869	John Thompson Hoffman*
1873	John A. Dix*
1875	Samuel Jones Tilden*
1877	Lucius Robinson
1880	Alonzo Cornell*
1883	Grover Cleveland
1885	Davis Bennett Hill
1892	Roswell Petibone Flower*
1895	Levi Parsons Morton
1897	Frank Swett Black
1899	Theodore Roosevelt
1901	Benjamin Barker Odell, Jr.
1905	Frank Weyland Higgins
1907	Charles Evans Hughes*
1910	Horace White
1911	John Alden Dix
1913	William Sulzer*
1913	Martin Henry Glynn
1915	Charles Seymour Whitman*
1919	Alfred E. Smith*
1921	Nathan L. Miller
1923	Alfred E. Smith*
1929	Franklin Delano Roosevelt
1933	Herbert H. Lehman*
1942	Charles Poletti*
1943	Thomas E. Dewey*
1955	William Averell Harriman
1959	Nelson A. Rockefeller
1973	Charles Malcom Wilson
1975	Hugh Carey*
1983	Mario Cuomo*
1995	George Pataki

* NYC residents

TALLEST BUILDINGS

World Trade Towers *1,350 ft*	1973
Empire State Building *1,250 ft*	1931
Chrysler Building *1,048 ft*	1929
Woolworth Building *792 ft*	1913
MetLife Tower *699 ft*	1909
Singer Building* *612 ft*	1908
Park Row Building *386 ft*	1899
St. Patrick's Cathedral *330 ft*	1888
Trinity Church *281 ft*	1846
St. Paul's Chapel *220 ft*	1794

* This building no longer exists.

NYC CATASTROPHES

The Great Fire	1776
Yellow Fever Epidemic	1803
Asiatic Cholera Epidemic	1832
The Great Fire	1835
Asiatic Cholera Epidemic	1849
The Astor Place Riot	1849
The Draft Riots	1863
The Windsor Hotel Fire	1899
The *General Slocum* Ferry Fire	1904
The Triangle Shirtwaist Fire	1911

NEW YORK FILE

FEATURED IN FICTION

The Age of Innocence
Edith Wharton *(1920)*

The Alienist
Caleb Carr *(1994)*

Banished Children of Eve
Peter Quinn *(1994)*

Bartleby the Scrivener
Herman Melville *(1853)*

The Bonfire of the Vanities
Tom Wolfe *(1987)*

Bright Lights, Big City
Jay McInerney *(1984)*

Butterfield 8
John O'Hara *(1935)*

The Fountainhead
Ayn Rand *(1943)*

From Time to Time
Jack Finney *(1995)*

Go Tell It on the Mountain
James Baldwin *(1953)*

Knickerbocker's History of New York
Washington Irving *(1809)*

The Prince of Central Park
E. H. Rhodes *(1975)*

Maggie: A Girl of the Streets
Stephen Crane *(1893)*

Manhattan Transfer
John Dos Passos *(1925)*

Ragtime
E. L. Doctorow *(1974)*

Simple Speaks His Mind
Langston Hughes *(1950)*

Stuart Little
E.B. White *(1945)*

Tales of Manhattan
Louis Auchincloss *(1967)*

Time and Again
Jack Finney *(1970)*

Washington Square
Henry James *(1880)*

The Waterworks
E. L. Doctorow *(1994)*

Winter's Tale
Marc Helprin *(1983)*

STARRING IN FILM

After Hours (1985)

Annie Hall (1977)

The Apartment (1960)

Barefoot in the Park (1967)

Billy Bathgate (1991)

The Bowery (1933)

Breakfast at Tiffany's (1961)

Broadway Danny Rose (1984)

The Cotton Club (1984)

Crossing Delancey (1988)

Die Hard With a Vengeance (1995)

42nd Street (1933)

Ghostbusters (1984)

The Godfather (1972)

Grand Central Murder (1942)

King Kong (1933)

Manhattan (1979)

Manhattan Melodrama (1934)

Manhattan Murder Mystery (1993)

Mean Streets (1973)

Metropolitan (1990)

Midnight Cowboy (1969)

Miracle on 34th Street (1947)

Moonstruck (1987)

New York, New York (1977)

The Odd Couple (1967)

The Out-of-Towners (1970)

The Pawnbroker (1965)

Prince of the City (1981)

The Producers (1968)

Rear Window (1954)

Rosemary's Baby (1968)

Sweet Smell of Success (1957)

Taxi Driver (1976)

The Thin Man (1934)

Wall Street (1987)

When Harry Met Sally... (1989)

Working Girl (1988)

NEW YORK FILE

WALKING TOURS

Big Onion Walking Tours
439-1090

Municipal Arts Society
457 Madison Avenue
935-3960

Museum of the City of New York
1220 Fifth Avenue
534-1672, ext. 206

National Academy of Design
1083 Fifth Avenue
369-4880

New York City Cultural Walking Tours
285 Avenue C
979-2388

New York University
50 West 4th Street
998-7130

92nd Street Y
1395 Lexington Avenue
415-5628

Sidewalks of New York
320 West 65th Street
517-0201

Urban Park Rangers
Central Park
427-4040

MORE INFORMATION

Archives
(New York City)
31 Chambers Street
374-4781

Citybooks
61 Chambers Street
669-8245

Cooper Union for the Advancement
of Science and Art (Continuing
Education)
Cooper Square
353-4195

Ellis Island Museum of Immigration
Ellis Island
363-7620

Museum of the City of New York
1220 Fifth Avenue
534-1672

New York Bound Bookshop
50 Rockefeller Center Plaza
245-8503

New-York Historical Society
170 Central Park West
873-3400

New York Transit Museum
Schermerhorn Street, Brooklyn
718-330-3060

Reference and Resources
(New York City)
31 Chambers Street
788-8590

Urban Center Books
(Municipal Arts Society)
457 Madison Avenue
935-3592

NEW YORK FILE

GREAT VIEWS OF MANHATTAN

Brooklyn Bridge
City Hall Park

Central Park Reservoir
Central Park at 90th Street

Circle Line
Pier 83, West 42nd Street
563-3200

Empire State Building
Fifth Avenue at 34th Street
736-3100

Helicopter Services
East 60th Street and York Avenue
832-4510

Helicopter Sightseeing Tours
East 34th Street and the East River
683-4575

Liberty Helicopter Tours
West 30th Street and the Hudson River
967-6464

Rainbow Room Restaurant
30 Rockefeller Plaza
632-5100

River Cafe Restaurant
1 Water Street, Brooklyn
718-522-5200

Riverside Church Tower
Riverside Drive at 121st Street
222-5900

Roosevelt Island Tramway
Second Avenue and 60th Street
832-4543

Staten Island Ferry
Battery Park
718-390-5253

Terrace Restaurant
400 West 119th Street
666-9490

Top of the Sixes Restaurant
666 Fifth Avenue
757-6662

Top of the Tower Restaurant
(Beekman Tower Hotel)
3 Mitchell Place
980-4796

World Trade Center Observation Deck
World Trade Center
435-4170

Gargoyle, 18 Irving Place, 1924

NEW YORK FILE

THE ESSENTIAL NYC LIBRARY

Encyclopedia of New York. Yale University Press. 1995.

Diamondstein, Barbaralee. *The Landmarks of New York II.* Abrams, 1993.

Kouwenhoven, John A. *The Columbia Historical Portrait of New York.* Doubleday, 1953

Silver, Nathan. *Lost New York.* Houghton Mifflin, 1967.

Willensky, Elliot, and Norval White. *AIA Guide to New York City.* Harcourt Brace Jovanovich, 1988.

Wright, Carol von Pressentin. *Blue Guide to New York.* W. W. Norton, 1991.

BIBLIOGRAPHY

Ashton, Dore. *World Cultural Guide, New York.* Holt, Rinehart and Winston, 1972.

Bailey, Vernon Howe. *Magical City: Intimate Sketches of New York.* Charles Scribner's, 1935.

Berger, Meyer. *Meyer Berger's New York.* Random House, 1960.

Berman, Eleanor. *Eyewitness Travel Guide: New York.* Dorling Kindersley Ltd., 1993.

Black, Mary. *New York City's Gracie Mansion.* J. M. Kaplan Fund, 1984.

Bolton, Reginald P. *The Path of Progress.* Central Savings Bank, 1928.

Bonner, William. *New York, The World's Metropolis.* Polk, 1925.

Boyer, M. Christine. *Manhattan Manners, Architecture and Style, 1850-1900.* Rizzoli, 1985.

Brierly, J. (comp.) *The Streets of Old New York: Twenty-four scenes and stories originally appearing in the Antiques section of the* New York Sun, 194?.

The Brooklyn Museum. *American Renaissance, 1876-1917.* Brooklyn Museum,1979.

Brown, Henry Collins. *Valentine's Manual of Old New York.* Valentine's Manual, Inc., 1927 (and 1923).

Caro, Robert. *The Power Broker: Robert Moses and the Fall of New York.* Vintage Books, 1975.

City Inspector's Report, 1848.

Club Men of New York, 1888-1894.

Club Men of New York, 1893. The Republic Press, 1893.

Crimmins, John Daniel. *Irish-American Historical Miscelleny.* J. D. Crimmins, 1905.

NEW YORK FILE

Dolkart, Andrew S. *Guide to New York City Landmarks.* The Preservation Press, 1992.

Doman, James. *St. Nicholas Historic District.* New York Housing & Development Committee, 1973.

Duffy, John. *A History of Public Health in New York City, 1625-1866.* Russell Sage Foundation, 1868.

Dunshee, Kenneth Holcomb. *As You Pass By.* Hastings House Publishers, 1952.

Early, Elenor. *New York Holiday.* Rinehart & Co., 1950.

Ellis, Edward Robb. *The Epic of New York City.* Coward-McCann, 1966.

Emerson, Caroline Dwight. *New York City: Old and New.* Dutton, 1953.

Fitch, James Marston. *American Building: The Historical Forces That Shaped It.* Houghton Mifflin, 1973.

Footner, Hulbert. *New York, City of Cities.* J.B. Lippincott, 1932.

Furer, Howard. *New York: A Chronological and Documentary History, 1542-1970.* Oceania Publications, 1974.

Garraty, John A., and Peter Gay. *The Columbia History of the World.* Harper & Row, 1972.

Gayle, Margot, and Michel Cohen. *Manhattan's Outdoor Sculpture.* Prentice Hall, 1988.

Gold, Joyce. *From Trout Stream to Bohemia.* Old Warren Road Press, 1988.

Goldberger, Paul. *New York City Observed.* Vintage Books, 1979.

Goldstone, Harmon H. *History Preserved, A Guide to New York City Landmarks and Historic Districts.* Simon & Schuster, 1974.

Gordon, Mark. *Cue's Guide to Old New York.* North American Publishing Company, 1976.

Harper's Magazine. *New York.* Gallery Books, 1991.

Irwin, Wil. *Highlights of Manhattan.* Century, 1927.

King, Moses. *Notable New Yorkers.* M. King, 1899.

Klein, Carole. *Gramercy Park: An American Bloomsbury.* Ohio University Press, 1987.

Landmarks Preservation Committee. *Metropolitan Museum Historic District Designation Report,* Landmarks Preservation Commission, 1977.

Lankevich, George J., and Howard B. Furer. *A Brief History of New York City.* Associated Faculty Press, 1984.

Lederer, Joseph. *All Around the Town.* Charles Scribner's, 1975.

Letts, Vanessa. *Cadogan City Guides: New York.* Cadogan Books, 1993.

Lowe, David G. *New York, New York: An American Heritage Extra.* American Heritage Publishing Co., 1968.

NEW YORK FILE

Lyman, Susan. *The Story of New York, an Informal History of the City.* Crown Publishers, 1964.

McCullough, David G. *The Great Bridge.* Simon & Schuster, 1972.

Metropolitan Museum Historic District Designation Report. Landmarks Preservation Committee, 1977.

Morris, Lloyd. *Incredible New York.* Random House,1951.

Moscow, Henry. *The Street Book: An Encyclopedia of Manhattan's Street Names and Their Origins.* Hagstrom Company, 1978.

Moscow, Henry. *The Book of New York Firsts.* Collier Macmillan, 1982.

Murphy, Richard. *History of the Society of the Friendly Sons of St. Patrick's in the City of New York.* J. C. Dillon Company, 1962.

Old Buildings of New York. Brentanos, 1907.

Oppel, Frank. *Gaslight New York Revisited.* Castle Books, 1989.

Patterson, Samuel White. *Famous Men and Places in New York City.* Noble, 1923.

Peterson, A. E. *Landmarks of New York.* City History Club of New York, 1923.

Pine, John. *Seal and Flag of the City of New York, 1665-1915.* G. P. Putnam's Sons, 1915.

Placzek, Adolf. *Macmillan Encyclopedia of Architects.* Collier Macmillan, 1982.

Reed, Henry Hope. *The Golden City.* W. W. Norton, 1971.

Reynolds, Donald Martin. *Monuments and Masterpieces.* Macmillan, 1988.

The Architecture of New York City. Macmillan, 1984.

Riis, Jacob A. *How the Other Half Lives.* Charles Scribner's, 1903.

Rosensweig, Roy, and Elizabeth Blackmar. *The Park and the People.* Cornell University Press, 1992.

Schwartzman, Paul, and Rob Polner. *New York Notorious.* Crown Publishers, 1992.

Stokes, I. N. Phelps. *Iconography of Manhattan Island, 1498-1909.* Robert Dodd, 1926.

New York, Past and Present. 1524-1939. Plantin Press, 1939.

Tauranac, John. *Essential New York: A Guide to the History and Architecture of Manhattan's Important Buildings, Parks and Bridges.* Holt, Rinehart and Winston, 1979.

Van Pelt, Daniel. *Leslie's History of Greater New York.* Arkell Publishing Company, 1898.

White, Norval. *New York, A Physical History.* Atheneum, 1987.

Wolfe, Gerard R. *New York, Guide to the Metropolis.* McGraw-Hill, 1994.

INDEX